BOY GIRL—MAN WOMAN

BOY GIRL—

MAN WOMAN

Bent H. Claësson

with Photographs by Gregers Nielsen

Translated by Christine Hauch
Introduction by Michael Schofield

PERENNIAL LIBRARY
Harper & Row, Publishers
New York, Evanston, San Francisco, London

Originally published in Danish as *Dreng og pige mand og kvinde* by Hans Reitzels Forlag A/S, Copenhagen.

First published in English in Great Britain in 1971 by Calder & Boyars Ltd, London.

Illustrations on p. 98 kindly lent by Ramses and Abis Prevention. Illustrations on pp. 95, 101, 102, 105 by kind permission of the Consumers Association Contraceptive Supplement.

First PERENNIAL LIBRARY edition published 1975

LIBRARY OF CONGRESS CATALOG CARD NUMBER: 74–18112

STANDARD BOOK NUMBER: 06–080338-X

Contents

NOTE

Slight alterations in the book have been made by Beth Gutcheon to reflect American law and practices.

Introduction

Recently I have completed a research for the Health Education Council in which I traced some of the young people I saw seven years ago when I was writing the report on the sexual behavior of young people. They were eighteen then and now they are twenty-five, most are married, and many of them have children.

Almost all of them (97%) said that they wished they had been given more information about sex by their parents and at school. Less than one in three (28%) of those who received sex education had a good word for it; nearly half (41%) said it was quite useless.

Many of them felt that it was given too late—they had already learned the basic facts in other ways, and many of them sensed that it did not tell them what they really wanted to know. It becomes clear that when we set out to help young people to understand sex, we are more likely to go too slow than too fast, and we are more likely to be too timid than too frank.

This is something we might remember when we criticize those who wish to push ahead too fast. We may be going too fast for the aldermen and the bishops, but are we not going too slow for the children? And who, we might ask, are we doing the sex education for, the aldermen or the kids?

I also asked these young men and women: "Do you feel you know all you need to know about sex?" It is both amazing and shaming that a large number (40% men, 31% women) admitted that there were many gaps in their knowledge of sex. Various comments were made, but the main demand was for hard concrete factual information. The men wanted to know more about the women, the women more about the men; most of all, they wanted to learn how to help their partner to find more sexual satisfaction.

Two years ago when I suggested at a Family Planning conference that we should teach young people how to enjoy sexual activities, the press reacted with jokes about special "schools for sex." A leader in the *Daily Mail* asked indignantly, "Has Mr. Schofield considered the feelings of the poor boy who fails his 'O' levels at sex?"

It is a good question. Nine out of ten boys and girls leaving school would fail any exam about the symptoms of V.D.; most school-leavers would fail an exam about methods of birth control; and most boys and girls would fail an exam in the art of making love. Because sex is not something that just comes naturally; like all the best things in life, it is something that takes a bit of learning.

Here at last is a book that tells the young reader what he wants to know and what he needs to know. Nearly all young boys and girls are confused by strong sexual emotions that they want to understand and control. Here they will find the straightforward factual information they have been looking for, presented simply and sympathetically, without evasion.

In this book many young people will find the answers to questions they dare not ask in class. Frequently a question goes unasked in school because the adolescent does not know the polite words or, more unfortunately, because he genuinely does not want to shock his teacher. The author and translator of this book have not been afraid to use the simple crude words when it is necessary to be absolutely clear. On the other hand, there are other more acceptable words and it is not a bad idea for the young reader to learn them and use them so that he can ask questions and express opinions without shocking other people.

Regrettably, some people are going to be offended by certain paragraphs in this book. It can hardly be avoided when someone is trying to be truthful about sex because, alas, to some people even the truth is offensive.

I should particularly like to recommend this book to those who feel that the so-called permissive society has got out of control and to those who feel engulfed by what the Germans call the sex wave—the nudity in the theater, the blue films, the pornography, the sex supermarkets, the strip clubs. I believe that all this commercial exploitation of sex is an inevitable, but temporary, phase—the price we have to pay for the past guilt-ridden attitude to sex. But all these excesses cannot compete with the real thing. If we can help our children to adopt a relaxed sensitive attitude to sex, they won't be interested in strip clubs or pornography. I hope we can teach them, and teach ourselves for that matter, that sex is only a small part of life, but a nice part, to be appreciated and enjoyed, but not something to be put on a pedestal and worshipped, and not something to be ashamed of and stifled.

The one sure barrier against the excesses of the sex wave is more and better sex education.

Michael Schofield, August, 1971
(Social psychologist and author of
The Sexual Behaviour of Young People)

Foreword

Especially for Parents and Teachers

The last twenty years or so have seen an increasing interest in sexual questions in the Western world—or perhaps it would be more accurate to say that the continually fermenting preoccupation with this vital topic has been allowed to bubble up to the surface, as the Victorian narrow-mindedness of the last century has lost its hold on common morality.

After Sigmund Freud's epoch-making work at the beginning of the century, the chief figure in this sexual breakthrough has undoubtedly been A. C. Kinsey, whose first scientific report, *Sexual Behavior in the Human Male* (1948), created a furor by demonstrating the enormous gap between the conventional morality of society as regards sexual topics and the private erotic behavior of the individual. In 1953 Kinsey published his second report, *Sexual Behavior in the Human Female*. Since then reports of sexual researches on the same lines as Kinsey's have been published all over the world, though no researcher has achieved anything comparable in scope—let alone in quality.

These and similar works of research are based on interviews or questionnaires. They describe what people do and have done, and in some cases show why. Strictly speaking they are only talking about a particular form of sexual behavior at a given time and place, which the person interviewed may distort out of modesty or slips of memory.

There have also been attempts to analyze ordinary sexual responses from a physiological point of view, though it was not until Masters and Johnson, in their *Human Sexual Response* (1966), carried out their searching experiments on voluntary subjects with the technical refinements of a laboratory that we obtained a clear picture of the changes taking place in the body during sexual intercourse. The radical methods used by these investigators in tackling the matter can be illustrated by a single example: in order to study the responses of the vagina and womb from inside they used a glass tube with an built-in movie-camera, thus solving a number of puzzles in an area otherwise abounding in sexual superstition.

Following in the wake of this kind of scientific research there have been some extremely fine books on sex education published in recent years. But these books are directed first and foremost at an adult audience whose experience gives them a basic understanding of comprehensive descriptions of sexual activity and the ability to put them into practice. With very few exceptions, our new knowledge has left no mark on books of sex instruction for the teen-ager—a lack that this book is attempting to make good.

Meanwhile, the point of sex education is not only to popularize the results of certain experiments, but also, and this is just as essential, to put the matter in perspective. In this respect the whole outlook and experience of the individual cannot help but determine the form and content of his teaching. Thus some people will feel that sex is so bound up with moral attitudes that one *must* take some kind of moral line, while others think that the more old-fashioned morality must gradually become totally irrelevant to any discussion of our sexual conduct.

I am in sympathy with the latter argument and I intend to refrain from any kind of moralizing in this book, though the sober-minded reader will see quite clearly that the book is making one moral point, namely, that the individual person should have the right to satisfy his sexual needs regardless of age, sex and—as long as there is no threat to the emotional or physical liberty of others—regardless of the form of expression taken by his sexual urge.

Apart from this Foreword, the book has been written first and foremost for young people, and this has determined the choice of vocabulary and pictorial material.* Some parents and teachers may therefore feel that I have failed in my duty to them, which is regrettable if understandable, but unavoidable if I am to fulfill my obligations to the young.

Some parents will doubtless feel that it is harmful for their teen-age children to know too much about sex—or at least that it is harmful to know it too soon. But there is no scientific proof that knowledge about sex is harmful, while observation has shown in a great many instances that ignorance, incomplete knowledge, or incorrect information about these matters can have serious consequences.

One of the things parents may be afraid of is that sexual knowledge of a more technical nature at too early an age may arouse and stimulate their children to the extent that they will throw themselves rashly into sexual relationships and will be forced to suffer the consequences. This is why many parents go out of their way to hide *their* sex manuals as soon as their children reach sexual maturity. But research has

---

*The original Danish edition employs more colloquial language. It also includes more explicit pictorial material.—The Publishers.

shown that the factors determining whether a child has his first erotic contact at an early age or later on are much less immediate than this. Statistics show that early puberty (the beginning of menstruation and ejaculation) determines an earlier start to sexual activity. But above all, it is a question of environment, social class, emotional contact in the home, school-leaving age, and so on. Comprehensive sex education probably has the opposite effect, making the first sexual contact less disturbing and confusing for the participant and, indirectly, one hopes, creating that confidence which is one of the requirements of young people starting to use contraceptives. In the following chapters we shall see how the sex instinct is already at work in childhood and comes to life completely during puberty and the years that follow. We shall study the different ways in which the sexual urge may be satisfied, explain a bit about what actually takes place during sexual stimulation and climax, and attempt to describe the difficulties that may complicate a sexual relationship, especially when you are young. I have devoted a fairly long chapter to methods of contraception, although I have no illusions that every reader will follow the advice. We must all accept that there are times when feelings and the sexual urge are too powerful for reason. But it would be absurd if an unwanted pregnancy were due to pure and simple ignorance. I then talk a little about infatuation and love, the abortion problem, and sexual minority groups. Finally, at the end of the book I have compiled a list in alphabetical order of the minor infirmities which may afflict young people and, with the advice of a doctor, I have supplied various remedies for tackling these problems.

There are several subjects I have hardly mentioned, like chromosomes, hormones, pregnancy and labor, since these are covered much more thoroughly in other books.

I would like to express my gratitude to Anders Groth, the psychiatrist, for his moral support and professional advice during the preparation of this text.

1. Sexuality in Children

The sexual instinct and urge are not phenomena that first become active during puberty.

We can already observe in infants how their hands will often move quite involuntarily toward the sex organs—something, by the way, that can also be seen in adults who have just woken up, either after ordinary sleep or after an anaesthetic. The infant, then, will play with his sex organs, and we must suppose that this fiddling brings a certain sense of well-being. Boys, at any rate, will frequently make their penis go stiff and both boys and girls may tickle themselves so strenuously that they become quite red in the face.

While they are still babies, children become conscious of which sex they belong to—as boys or girls— and for some time they may be totally absorbed in the interesting question of where the difference between the two lies. They compare themselves to adults, discover that one day they are going to be just like mommy or daddy; but there the comparison remains—impertinent and inquisitive. On investigation, children realize how nice it is to be tickled "on the bottom"—and by someone else. Even so, their games are never protracted, as they so often are in later childhood, though there is no doubt that young children can be sexually attracted and express their feelings for one another.

Many babies, especially little boys, will have phases of walking round fiddling quite openly with their sex organs, sometimes so intensively that one might think they were masturbating. Usually this has no significance, but frequent fiddling may, just like continuous thumb-sucking, be a sign that something is wrong with the child's adjustment to his parents, family, and friends.

School children, from the age of seven until puberty, may be deeply interested in the opposite sex. They sometimes talk about emotional, childish infatuations, and little boys and girls try to go to bed with one another.

Many games, moreover, may have a sexual quality: doctors and nurses, for example. Here the intention is obviously to create a play situation in which the children are *allowed* to see and feel each other's sex organs.

Adults react very differently to the sexual play of children. It is, however, being recognized that sexuality plays an important and natural part in a child's life. It is one of the many ways in which a child uses games to prepare himself for adult life. A warm, open, and tolerant attitude on the part of parents and elder brothers and sisters toward the child's interest and pleasure in sexual play can therefore determine the child's later sexual and emotional development.

2. Puberty and the Years That Follow

Puberty is the name given to that period of our lives lasting several years, when we cross the bridge from childhood to the adult world. You can be so deeply conscious of the physical and mental changes taking place in yourself that after a few years it is hard to recognize yourself, just as other people may fall about in astonishment that it really is little Peter or Jane who has changed *so* much.

Early or Late Development

There is a wide variety in the ages at which individual people reach puberty.

On average, girls are sexually mature a year or so earlier than boys. Thus for girls puberty starts at around eleven to thirteen years, as opposed to boys, for whom puberty does not begin until they are twelve to fourteen years old. In a small minority of girls the first signs of puberty may even be noticeable as early as nine years old, or conversely as late as seventeen. Similarly, there may be great variations in the ages at which boys enter the first phases of puberty, from eleven to eighteen years old.

If puberty starts early and is accompanied by considerable growth, you will also stop growing earlier —on average it is four to six years from the beginning of puberty to full height. Hereditary conditions determine how tall or short you are in the end, just as the time at which puberty starts is also supposed to be a question of heredity. Good, varied food is a necessity if you want to grow and develop the potential you have inherited from your parents. It is the improved diet of the average young person of today, together with extra vitamins, that is chiefly responsible for his or her being taller and more sexually mature at a slightly earlier age than young people were a hundred years ago.

Physical Changes

At the beginning of puberty the arms, legs, neck, trunk, and sex organs all start to grow. Growth can take place either gradually or in leaps and bounds, and only rarely affects the whole body equally. On the contrary, the arms, legs, and neck usually grow faster than the trunk, and boys especially can become so bony and lanky that it is hard to find clothes to fit them—and parents are often reluctant to pay very much for their clothes because they know that it will not be long before their children have grown out of them.

When the muscles and bones develop in boys, they want to try out their new strength. They may begin to get a growth of beard and for some this can present a real problem. Should they begin to shave? On the one hand, they may be shy about their downy faces, hoping that no one has noticed, while on the other hand, they are secretly proud of this sign of virility.

Both boys' and girls' voices break. Boys may take some time to find their bass pitch and their voices may break easily, especially when they are shouting. Girls' voices also become a little deeper, acquiring more fullness and tone. These changes are due to the growth of the vocal chords and the larynx. This is more evident in boys, in whom the projection of the larynx on the neck is called the Adam's apple.

Girls' figures become more rounded, as a layer of fat settles under the skin. The pelvis grows and widens, so that it can fulfill its later function as a channel during birth. Some girls may also have slight growth of hair on the face. This is almost always due to hereditary factors and not to illness. If you are very embarrassed about having hair "in the wrong places" you can easily get rid of it either by electrolysis or other cosmetic methods, but be sure to get medical advice on this, since hair tends to grow thicker after having been plucked or shaved.

The most absorbing aspect of physical change in puberty can be the growth of the sex organs, disturbing on one hand, but very exciting on the other. In boys, the penis grows larger and thicker and darker-skinned, and strange new sensations can be felt in it. It is gradually assuming the characteristics of what is also a fertilizing organ. The scrotum and the balls grow at the same time and the scrotum becomes darker in color. Internally, the prostate gland, the spermatic cord, and the seminal vesicles also grow.

The sex organs of girls develop toward their mature form in the same way. The breasts grow and the nipples become larger and darker. Often one breast develops more quickly than the other. Some girls get a very big bosom and may feel shy about it, though usually the size will decrease again over the next few years. Other girls brood because they think that their breasts are developing too slowly; but I can assure you that being erotically exciting and able to suckle children bears no relation to the size of the breasts.

Besides, fashions change, so that the bosom is supposed to be big and buxom one year and almost invisible the next.

For a girl the question of whether to begin wearing a brassiere may become a problem. It can be unpleasant to have "flapping" breasts—when you run downstairs, for example; it may even be painful. Obviously a bra is going to help, only you must remember that it must not be too tight or the breasts will not be able to grow freely. It has become fashionable for many young girls not to wear a bra and this is supposed to strengthen the muscles of the breast and reduce the tendency to a fallen bosom.

Some boys may also experience some minor development of the breasts, but this always disappears again quickly, so you need not be worried or embarrassed by it.

The clitoris and the labia become larger. In some girls the inner labia may become visible between the outer. Internally the vagina, the womb, the fallopian tubes, and the ovaries are all developing (see pages 21–24).

In both sexes hair appears under the arms and around the sex organs, and, more especially in boys, on various other parts of the body. In addition, the composition of one's sweat changes, the tendency to sweat becomes more pronounced and thus body odor becomes more powerful (see page 139). The skin and hair begin to get greasy and many young people develop blackheads and pimples. Spots can be an unbearable torture, as they make you feel so repulsive. You find that you do not even dare dance cheek to cheek or cuddle up to someone you fancy in case he or she will be disgusted by touching you. You will find some advice on this problem on pages 135–136.

Sexual Maturity

When a girl has her first period and a boy his first ejaculation, we say that they have reached sexual maturity. Exactly what this means is explained in the next chapter, on the sex organs. They are, however, signs that a girl can have children and a boy can make a girl pregnant.

For boys sexual maturity means that the semen is emptied out at more or less regular intervals. This may either happen involuntarily, most often during sleep, or voluntarily, as a result of masturbation, petting, or intercourse.

Involuntary, nocturnal ejaculation may be accompanied by erotic dreams. The first time it happens, the dream may seem like the bed-wetting dream of a child, but it soon acquires a more sexual content.

Some boys may be worried because they leave telltale marks on pajamas and bedclothes. But this is nothing to be ashamed about. Wet dreams are quite natural—and your parents know this.

Although the sperm is being continually produced inside the body, wet dreams will decrease or disappear altogether, depending on how often you masturbate.

If you are absolutely determined to hide this particular sign of puberty from your parents, you can always masturbate before bedtime or go to bed with your underpants on, since they are usually quite a bit tighter than pajama trousers and therefore more likely to absorb the sperm so that none leaks out and stains the sheets. Then the next morning you can wash out your underpants in cold water with a little toilet soap.

As we have said, sexual maturity in girls is indicated by the first period. This may be accompanied by sexual dreams and erotic feelings and sometimes by fear and disgust. It is better for a girl if she can discuss this with a friend or relative, especially if she feels faint or weak around this time.

Unfortunately there are cases where the first period comes as a shock to a young girl, especially if she has reached sexual maturity early and has therefore not come across similar experiences among her classmates, or if her parents have put off the embarrassment of telling her what would happen, thinking there was still plenty of time.

Emotional Changes

During the teens an unbelievable amount of psychological changes are taking place. The adult world is opening out before you and a number of things you have never even dreamed of suddenly become full of meaning. On the one hand, you are conscious of disturbing signals from your growing body, and on the other, you are perceiving and adjusting to the people around you, who also seem changed, both because you are looking at them with new eyes and because adults really are changing their attitude toward you.

You may fall in love for the first time and while the feeling lasts you may find it impossible to think about anything else. The other person will be in your thoughts day and night and you may feel such an overwhelming desire to be with him or her that you will put everything else aside to meet this need. But there is a risk that being in love will not last forever. If you are unlucky there will come a day when the whole thing is broken off and you feel as if you will never be happy again. Life may seem to have lost all meaning for you. But luckily the self-preservation

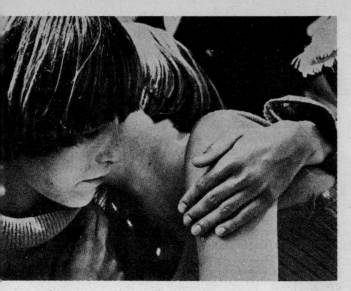

It is hard to think about anything else when you are in love.

instinct wins through and after a while the whole thing will be forgotten—well, nearly, because such a powerful experience leaves its mark on the memory and may later form part of your knowledge of the world.

At other times your imagination and intellect becomes totally caught up in all sorts of new problems, theoretical and practical—it is like going on a voyage of discovery to a new land.

But there is also the discovery that you are a member of a society that imposes its own particular demands. Suddenly you have to decide what attitude you are going to adopt toward education and work, while life at school makes greater demands on your mind. At first some young people find all these things so overpowering and confusing that they may try to prolong the secure refuge of childhood by concealing from the people around them the signs that they are entering adulthood.

It Is Hard to Be an Odd Man Out

Friends play a fantastically important part in the growth to maturity and for this reason it can be very hard to either an early or late developer.

Early developers may come in for some teasing from the rest of their class, though this is basically due to envy. It may be said that you have hidden admirers, but if you remember that this is something to be proud of rather than ashamed about, such teasing will be easier to bear.

It can be even worse to feel that you are the smallest—a child among grown-ups. The kind of teasing you are subjected to then can become so intolerable that it might be an idea to find some way of changing your group of friends so that you have a chance to achieve a better position in a new circle of people.

Finding Your Real Self

Most young people will feel a strong sense of involvement with a particular crowd of friends, and this group will be of great significance in the later development of the individual. While beginning to form some opinions about who and what you are, you may well attach a great deal of importance to what your friends think of you and try to copy them, in both appearance and behavior, so that you will not be considered different or thrown out of the group.

These considerations obviously play an important part in the formation of different attitudes and responses to sexual matters. If you belong to a group of friends in which the others have already had some sexual experience, or say they have, it immediately seems very important that you should try yourself— even if you are terribly unsure and possibly do not even want to yet.

Quite often you may have to join another group of people, because you have perhaps moved, changed schools, left school, changed your job, or been abandoned by the group you were in before. But you may also decide of your own free will to change your circle of friends because you find that your ideas differ from their on an increasing number of topics —of which sex may be one.

Changing groups voluntarily because you no longer find any satisfaction in belonging or being thrown out of a group because the others cannot accept your views on some subject or another are signs that you are beginning to find your own way in the world.

Possibly, in private, you will stand in front of a mirror "posing," in order to find out who you really are. You may be so spellbound by a filmstar, a pop idol, an adult, or a friend you admire that you practice being as like them as you can, imitating voice, gestures, facial expression, clothes, and so on.

After a while the role you are playing may feel identical to your own personality, until eventually you grow tired of it because you realize that it did not totally express what you really are.

You may change roles several times, often a necessary part of trying to pinpoint what your true self is.

Obviously the roles you have most success with will be the most difficult to drop—even if they reflect only a minor part of your character and potential. This kind of clinging to security is undoubtedly one of the chief reasons why many adults remain dependent throughout their lives on the role that they

11

think makes them most popular and that ties them most strongly to the group they find most attractive.

This is, of course, a danger to the development of personality on an individual level, and to democracy on a social level. Role-playing is one of the main reasons behind the formation of mass opinion and prejudice and thus also behind the creation of irreconcilable hatred between the great cultural divisions of the world.

Once you have reached your twenties, therefore, both for your own sake and for the sake of society, you ought to settle accounts with your group of friends in the sense that you try to determine how many of the attitudes shared by the group are also basically your own. At the same time you should make up your mind whether you are prepared to sacrifice personal freedom and independence in order to tie yourself to any one particular, biased role, which it may be impossible to discard once you have been playing it for ten or twenty years.

Scruples of this kind may also lead individual, more mentally mature, teen-agers to break with their friends and stop playing roles in an attempt to be themselves—for good or evil.

Parental Problems

In most societies parents are deeply interested in their children's transition from the world of the child to that of the adult, of which the parents are after all the closest representatives. It is thus quite common for them to protect their child from the sort of initiation process that would admit the child to an adult "mystery"—sometimes of a sexual nature (see, for example, the section on Homosexuality).

At various times during your teens, at birthdays,

for example, adults may tell you that you are getting to be a real grown-up, but they rarely mean what they say. In any case it is only in exceptional cases that you will see them accepting the consequences of their words.

Young people halfway through puberty may not necessarily feel particularly grown-up. Yet the increasing development of consciousness and the strange transformations taking place in the body point the way to the promised land of the adult. So, for many of them, it becomes important to act *more* grown-up than they really are. This boosts self-confidence but undoubtedly creates many problems. They start consciously asserting their new-found independence—often adopting the opinions of friends or adults they admire.

Through your new—adult—eyes, you can see more and more clearly that the adult world is not all that perfect; it is full of prejudice and narrow-minded rules. And this sharpens your sense of criticism, so that you soon find yourself in conflict with your parents, among others. What you may find it hard to realize is that many grown-ups are also unhappy, insecure, and disappointed people, who can only cope with life by maintaining the traditional parental position of authority, upholding futile rules and a facade of idyllic perfection in front of their children because of their own fears.

Many parents of course feel justifiable concern for their children's welfare. They may have had bitter experiences themselves and can hardly bear to see their children repeating their own mistakes. But experience is not always something that can be read about or dictated. It should penetrate the body so that it can filter through and become—well, just experience.

Many women who are tied to the home, and parents who have lost their partners through death or divorce, find that life suddenly seems to have lost its purpose. So they cling to their adolescent children, by restricting their freedom and rights—or by falling into self-pity and "illness" that indirectly tie the children to them.

Other parents may become thoroughly jealous—they can see their children living an apparently irresponsible, free and easy life in a luxury they never knew when they were children. Everyone knows the expression "Now, when I was young . . ."

Whatever the reason, it remains that relations between parents and teen-age children are often intolerable. The economic dependence that our society tends to impose on young people, and which can be as much of a strain for parents as for children, only increases the difficulties. Many of you may have had remarks like "You're treating home more and more like a hotel" flung at you by an infuriated father or mother; and they may be both right and wrong.

Parents could do a great deal themselves to improve the kind of contact they have with their children, above all by being more fair-minded, making allowances for mistakes and uncertainties, and including young people in their adult lives as neutrally and instructively as they can, without any petty moralizing.

And young people, on their side, could try to put themselves in their parents' position a bit more, making an effort to see them as people with good and bad points.

Even with good will on both sides, agonizing moments of conflict can arise, but these encounters contribute toward making the young into detached and independent people. They are a necessary stage in the process of mental development.

Youth and Society

In the animal kingdom we can observe how animals begin to reproduce as soon as they reach sexual maturity. It is important for the survival of the species. Among humans, also, there was a time when sexual maturity meant the beginning of sexual display and reproduction. In some states of the U.S.A. it is still legally possible for girls to be married at the age of twelve and boys at fourteen, though admittedly it happens very rarely. In the Far East, however, it is still common in many places for girls to be married when they are that young.

In America, both partners have to reach an "age of consent" before they can get married without their parents' permission. The legal age varies from state to state, the most common being eighteen. Furthermore, it is illegal to have intercourse with someone under the age of consent.

These regulations show quite clearly how society has changed its attitudes, so that it is no longer considered desirable for sexual maturity to be the natural start to sexual experience and its consequences. These stringent terms are intended to protect the young against the burden of motherhood or fatherhood at too early an age, and to prevent the birth of too many children into an emotionally insecure and economically unstable environment.

This protective attitude has developed as society has changed into what we call a highly civilized industrial society, one that has an increasing need for its citizens to be educated to perform special tasks.

Our "apprenticeship" to society has become more and more protracted, so that we may now have to wait between two and twelve years after we have reached sexual maturity before we are economically in a position to settle down and support our children satisfactorily.

But during this apprenticeship we have powerful sexual urges that need to be relieved in some way or other, and for boys these urges are at their strongest during those very years when it is most difficult for them to find a satisfactory outlet.

In the chapter on masturbation we mention that almost all boys and some girls masturbate during this time. This common form of release may be satisfying enough for some years, but there comes a point, which varies a great deal from person to person, when many people find themselves in the predicament of wanting for one reason or another to have an affair with a person whom they find attractive.

You will always find some adults who don't want you to. They think that you are too young and should wait either until you are married or at least until you are well and truly engaged, since an engagement is seen by most people as being just as binding as marriage. Then, if anything goes wrong, you can be quickly piloted into marriage.

Luckily other people are more liberal in their attitude, but some young men and even more young girls may find it difficult to make up their minds, possibly because they are afraid of condemnation by their elders or worried about becoming pregnant and being left to bear the responsibility on their own, and because through their upbringing they have inherited some of the more staid moral ideas of the adult world.

The problem is greater for girls because for some

reason we do not allow them the same freedom of sexual development as we do boys. Young men can "sow their wild oats," whereas a girl who tries to do the same sort of thing is immediately branded as "loose" or even as a "slut." Many young men who have exercised no self-restraint but tried a bit of everything may find it hard in their heart of hearts to accept a girl who has lived as they have. In fact women still do not have sexual equality with men, far from it.

Obviously no one is saying that you grow very much wiser sexually or otherwise by "flitting from flower to flower"—on the contrary, the desire to do this may betray an inner fickleness and superficiality —but it seems sad that boys are allowed to have what they want whereas girls are subjected to the criticism of an outdated and lukewarm morality if they follow the same path.

But this kind of prejudice is difficult to shake off. It is always worth keeping a self-critical watch on yourself for a tendency to be carried away in the condemnation of another girl.

How Early Do Others Go to Bed with Each Other —and Why?

Investigations have shown that nearly all young people think that their friends have had more sexual experience than they have. Although some statistical evidence of sexual experience among young people does exist, it is not entirely reliable. The figures represent all social classes, and there are several factors involved in whether you belong to a group of people who pull the average down or push it up: your background, the kind of emotional contact you have with your parents, and the number of years' education you have received, to name but a few. Thus generally speaking, a young person who has good relations with his parents and a tradition in the family of pursuing higher education will have less sexual intercourse than someone of the same age who has less good relations with his parents and whose family have always left school at an early age. Between these two extremes, there exist endless combinations of the different factors and these will constitute the largest group and the one that lies closest to the average figure. Researches into the situation show that only a small percentage of young people under sixteen have experienced intercourse. Of young people under seventeen an average of less than half of young men have tried intercourse as opposed to considerably fewer young girls.

Little is known also about the reasons why young people first have sexual intercourse. Admitting that such classifications are oversimplified, however, it is probably true to say that about half of all young men and a higher proportion of girls first have intercourse because they are in love or feel some kind of emotional involvement with their partner; the others do so out of curiosity. And the younger they are at the time of their first sexual experience the more often they are prompted by curiosity.

3. The Sex Organs

THE FEMALE SEX ORGANS

The female sex organs are divided into the outer organs, which can be seen from outside, and the inner organs, which are hidden in the lower half of the abdomen.

The Outer Sex Organs

We include here the labia majora and minora, the maidenhead or hymen, the clitoris, and the mons veneris. One can also regard the breasts as outer organs.

The hymen is a little crease of membrane that partly covers the entrance to the vagina. It usually breaks during a girl's first intercourse, though it may also happen if she uses internal tampons during menstruation. Breaking the hymen can cause a certain amount of soreness and bleeding, but these are usually insignificant and certainly nothing to be afraid of.

The entrance to the vagina is surrounded by the labia minora, which end in front in the clitoris, and these labia minora are partly covered by the labia majora, which are carried right out into the mons veneris. Beneath the clitoris lies the opening to the urethra; and below the entrance to the vagina, the anus. The clitoris, or more accurately, the tip of the clitoris, is the most sensitive part of the woman, as responsive to touch as the tip of the penis, and is therefore also the most important organ of passion

19

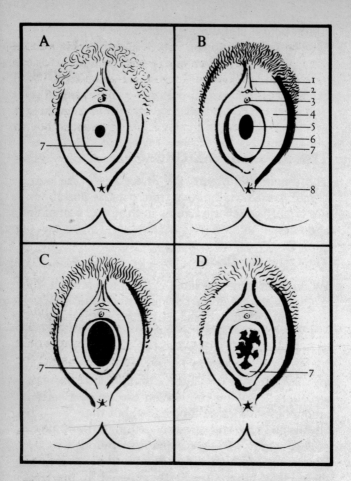

Figures A, B, C, D show the different shapes the hymen may take. 1. The body of the clitoris. 2. The tip of the clitoris. 3. The opening of the urethra. 4. The labia minora. 5. The opening of the vagina. 6. The labia majora. 7. The hymen. 8. The anus.

In figure C the hymen is so small and the opening of the vagina so large that a tampon can be used without any difficulty.

both before and during intercourse.

The size of both the clitoris and the labia minora may vary greatly from one girl to another, just as the right and left labia are rarely the same size. These differences have no importance as far as sexual relations are concerned, though right in the beginning it may be more awkward for an inexperienced boy to find a small clitoris than a large one.

Between the labia an odorous, whitish, waxy secretion is produced.

The Breasts

Development of the breasts is one of the signs that you have reached puberty.

As you know, the breast has two functions. The most important one is suckling children. Soon after the woman has given birth the glands contained in the breasts start producing milk to feed the child. The other function is a sexual one. Both the sight and the feel of the naked breast stimulate a strong erotic response in the man, and the nipples are among the most sexually sensitive parts of the woman.

The Inner Sex Organs

These include the vagina, the womb, the fallopian tubes, and the ovaries.

The vagina is a cleft, three and a half to four inches long, with very elastic walls that can be stretched enormously wide, as they have to be during childbirth. The walls of the vagina are covered with a fluted, mucous membrane (like a washboard) that is of importance during intercourse when the uneveness intensifies the sensations in the man.

Right up near the end of the vagina it joins the womb, which is shaped remarkably like a pear. This

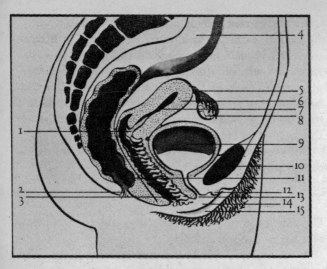

Above: the female internal sex organs (dissected length-wise). 1. The mouth of the womb. 2. The anus. 3. The vagina. 4. The rectum. 5. The left fallopian tube. 6. The womb. 7. The cavity of the womb. 8. The left ovary. 9. The

"pear" is turned on its head with the thinnest part, "the stalk," protruding a little way down into the vagina. This stalk is called the cervix and is hollow, so that a tiny passage, the cervical canal, leads up into the interior of the womb. The cervical canal is very narrow, so you need have no fear that a diaphragm or anything else for that matter will be able to disappear up it. The womb, or uterus, is also hollow and is lined with a mucous membrane to which a fertilized egg will become attached—once there it develops links with the blood vessels on the walls of the womb and grows into an embryo. The egg reaches the womb by way of two ducts, the fallopian tubes, that lead into the top of the womb from the ovaries. The ovaries are about the same size as a walnut and lie on each side of the abdomen right down over the groin. They are, in fact, small "factories" producing hormones and eggs. These hormones are chemical substances that affect, among other things, the monthly bleeding and the ability of the womb to keep the fertilized egg firmly lodged inside it. The ovaries also act as a store for the eggs. In sexually mature women one egg is released from one of the ovaries every twenty-six to thirty days, a process

bladder. 10. The pubic bone. 11. The rectum. 12. The clitoris. 13. The opening of the urethra. 14. The labia minora. 15. The labia majora.

Below: The female internal sex organs (dissected across). 1. The two ovaries; the one on the left of the picture has been dissected. 2. The two fallopian tubes; the one on the left of the picture has been dissected. 3. The cavity of the womb. 4. The womb. 5. The mouth of the womb. 6. The vagina, dissected and opened out; note the ribbed membrane.

known as ovulation, and is then carried along its fallopian tube down into the cavity of the womb. Incidentally ovulation may cause slight discomfort at the bottom of either the right or left side of the abdomen.

Fertilization

During intercourse the man squirts out his semen into the end of the vagina. His sperm cells are mobile and travel up through the cervical canal, on through the womb, and up into both fallopian tubes. If these cells encounter an egg, a single cell will burrow its way into the egg and it is then said that fertilization has taken place. The fertilized egg then becomes lodged in the mucous membrane that forms the lining of the womb. The woman is now pregnant and the period of nine months, during which the fetus develops into a baby capable of surviving on its own, is called a pregnancy.

Twins

If the fertilized egg divides into two at an early stage, each half can develop into a separate fetus. This causes what we call one-egg, or identical, twins. In some women two mature eggs are released at the same time and if both are fertilized and then become lodged in the womb they will develop into two fetuses. This causes two-egg, or fraternal, twins, who are not identical in looks.

Menstruation

If the egg is not fertilized, it will roll down into the vagina and slip out unnoticed. In the meantime the membrane of the lining of the womb will have grown thick and rich in food content, an ideal "nest" for the fertilized egg. If the egg is not fertilized this membrane comes away from the wall of the womb. As the membrane is shed a few of the small blood vessels in the womb break, but there is much less bleeding than you may think and what comes away is membrane dyed by blood. This flows down into the vagina and out of it. The process is know as menstruation (monthly period, "the curse") and may last for between three and nine days, though usually between four and six days.

When menstruation is finished the membrane begins to grow again and about fourteen days before the first day of the next period a new egg is released from the ovaries. From one menstruation to the next there is an interval of between twenty-six and thirty days. It continues in the same way for an average of thirty-five years, from between the ages of twelve to thirteen (nine to seventeen at the extreme) until a woman reaches forty to fifty-five and enters the change of life, or menopause.

Quite often young girls have a certain amount of bother with menstruation. The first year or so it can be irregular and cause pain in the abdomen. Although these troubles are not connected with disease of any kind, for practical reasons they are dealt with in the chapter on disease.

Hygiene during Menstruation

During your period it is important to keep yourself clean around the sex organs. Any blood and membrane that is not washed away every day will begin to decay and smell. An unhygienic person soon gets used to her own smell but may offend the people around her (just think how quickly you become insensitive to the smell of your own bowel movements, but if you go into a lavatory that someone else has just used you almost have to hold your nose).

To absorb the blood you can either use sanitary napkins or tampons. Sanitary napkins can be used by everybody, but they feel a bit bulky under tight-fitting trousers or a bathing suit and may restrict your movements. Tampons are put up into the vagina and swell as they absorb the blood. Outside your clothes no one can see whether you are using a tampon and you are free to take part in gymnastics, to dance, and so on. Tampons, however, because they do swell, may be difficult to get out if you are still a virgin.

If you break the hymen while you are trying to take a tampon out you can at least be glad that *that* is over. If the tampon seems to be hopelessly stuck a doctor will soon be able to take it out. Both napkins and tampons must be changed frequently, the stronger the bleeding the more often, possibly several times a day. There is a danger with tampons that you might forget to take them out, since you don't notice them. If the tampon remains inside you for several days, forgetting it may, in some unfortunate cases, cause an infection of the abdomen.

THE MALE SEX ORGANS

The man's sex organs consist of the penis, the scrotum, which holds the two balls or testicles, two epididymises, two seminal ducts (vas deferens), two seminal vesicles, the prostate gland, and the urethra.

The penis is composed of spongy tissue. The top part is called the head, or gland, the rest is called the body, or shaft. The head of the penis is the most sensitive part of the man, as sensitive as the woman's clitoris. Usually the head is covered by a thick fold of skin, the foreskin, which can be drawn right back.

(For tightness of the foreskin, see page 134). Under the foreskin, an odorous, whitish, waxy secretion, called smegma, is produced. In America it is common to have the foreskin removed in a simple operation called circumcision.

The Scrotum and the Balls

The scrotum is a bag of thin, brownish (pigmented) skin with a scattered growth of hair. Inside, it is divided into two compartments, each one containing one ball. When exposed to the cold the scrotum shrinks, a phenomenon that can also be observed during powerful sexual excitement.

The balls are the size of small plums, firm and smooth. They are not always exactly the same size and the left one usually hangs a little lower than the right. They slip between the fingers (like marbles in your pocket) but are highly sensitive to pressure or being hit. It is important for girls to remember this so that they do not squeeze them too hard when they are sexually stimulated.

The balls are a "factory" producing both hormones and sperm cells. Production continues throughout the day and night regardless of whether or not the man is sexually active. The sperm cells are then stored in the epididymis, which lies outside the balls. Two pipes, the seminal ducts, the thickness of string, lead from the epididymis up into the abdomen and end in the prostate gland. The two seminal vesicles are lodged just behind the prostate glands and lead out into the seminal ducts. The sperm cells are carried along the ducts and into the seminal vesicles, where they are mixed with seminal fluid, which is produced in the prostate gland. This fluid is necessary for the mobility of the sperm cells. The finished

27

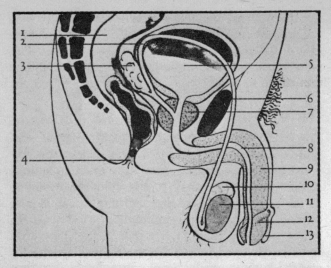

The male sex organs (dissected lengthwise). 1. The rectum. 2. The right spermatic duct. 3. The right seminal vesicle. 4. The anus. 5. The bladder. 6. The pubic bone. 7. The prostate gland. 8. The urethra. 9. Spongy tissue in the body of the penis. 10. The left epididymis. 11. The left testicle. 12. Spongy tissue in the head of the penis. 13. The foreskin.

semen is then pumped along the urethra, which runs through the prostate gland, and is finally squirted out through the opening of the urethra on the head of the penis. This process is called ejaculation.

Semen

Semen is a milky, slimy, sticky liquid with an insipid, slightly fishy smell. It is a little salty to the taste, with an aftertaste of vague bitterness. Semen is both sterile (bacteria-free) and nontoxic. It stains material but can be washed off with cold water and a little toilet soap.

About a teaspoonful of semen is released with each orgasm, though the more frequent the ejaculation, the less semen will be passed on each time. This amount of semen contains several hundred million sperm cells.

Erection

When the spongy tissue in the penis is filled with blood, it becomes longer, thicker, and firmer until it finally stands erect. This is then called an erection, a "hard-on" or a "stiff prick." Erection is usually due to some kind of erotic influence, though it can also be the result of other than immediately sexual causes. In puberty, especially, it can happen after very little irritation. The vibrations of some form of transport—for example, stomach exercises on a gym floor—even just the fear that it may happen, can cause the penis to stand revealingly away from the body. You may find this situation distressing and feel terribly embarrassed because you are not in control of what is happening. The best thing to do is concentrate on something completely different, or tense the stomach muscles to the breaking point, but if nothing helps you can always resort to going and masturbating in the toilet.

Another cause of involuntary erection is dreaming. Both aggressive and erotic dreams can produce an erection, though only sexual dreams will also lead to ejaculation. Waking up in the morning with a hard-on is thus due to the content of your dreams and not —as was until recently believed—to a full bladder.

Big or Small

There are countless misapprehensions as to the size of the penis. One of the things that keep these misunderstandings alive is that section of pornographic literature in which heavy-breasted women are described as being in hot pursuit of bigger and bigger pricks. But these books are mostly written by men, not women, and have very little to do with erotic reality. Although there can be great variations in the size of the limp penis from man to man, research has shown that these differences in size even out quite a bit with erection; so that what may seem a small penis when limp will become proportionately much larger when erect than what may seem a large penis when limp. Many young men, therefore, may be engaged in quite unnecessary speculation if they start drawing comparisons between their own small penises and others' larger ones. Besides, in fat men, part of the penis may be hidden by the fatty tissue around the pubic hair.

Of course there will be small differences—after all we are all built individually—but during intercourse these differences will even out because the woman's vagina adapts to the size of the penis so that it makes no difference to her pleasure whether the penis is slightly larger or smaller. For the same reason *she* need have no fear that the penis will be too big for her vagina—there will always be room unless the vagina is not sufficiently developed because the girl is not physically mature.

4. Masturbation

Masturbation comes from a Latin word meaning to rape with one's hand, so it can also mean something you do to someone else. It is also called onanism, a word stemming from the old biblical story about Onan, who was punished with death for refusing to give his dead brother children by impregnating his brother's widow. He interrupted intercourse with his sister-in-law by pulling out before ejaculation (the coitus interruptus method) and thus broke the prevailing law of the land.

The Christians of the Middle Ages were of the unhappy opinion that all sexual activity was sinful. So, in order to frighten young people away from self-gratification, they altered the story and told them that Onan had been condemned to death by God for the sin of masturbation. Since then self-gratification has been called onanism.

In previous centuries the attitude to masturbation has hardly been tolerant in Europe. In order to make young people feel guilty about this, books were written asserting that masturbation was a form of self-abuse that could lead to spinal consumption, brain fever, and madness. Small cages were also invented that fanatical parents could tie tightly round boys' genitals to prevent the "vice" from developing—and as if that were not enough, some of these cages were inlaid with sharp points or with ingenious alarm devices. In certain cases young girls suspected of self-gratification have had their clitoris removed by operation.

It goes without saying that these deliberate attempts to frighten have made life miserable for those countless people who continued to masturbate in spite of the terrifying prospects presented to them, making them anxious, ashamed, convinced of their own inferiority, and full of self-reproach.

It is therefore hard to overestimate the importance of the fact that in recent years so many researchers into sexual matters have concerned themselves with this problem and are all agreed that masturbation is completely harmless.

Masturbation Is Very Common

Research has shown that the majority of boys and young men masturbate from time to time, but it is not so widespread among girls. About half of them masturbate as a form of release from sexual urges and of those the majority begin either in connection with or following some other kind of sexual experience. It is reckoned that about three quarters of adult women have masturbated at one time or another.

These differences between the sexes have various causes. Firstly, boys and girls are differently brought up. Secondly, sexual maturity is indicated in different ways. Boys begin to experience involuntary nocturnal emission, which is accompanied by pleasurable sensations in the sex organs, whereas girls who begin to menstruate do not experience accompanying sexual feelings. Thirdly, the continuous production of semen in the balls gives rise to an underlying need for ejaculation. Finally, nature has made a boy's most sensitive part, the head of the penis, so accessible that it is continually exposed to irritation from clothes and fiddling from fingers, while a girl's most sensitive part, the clitoris, is protected by the labia. Thus boys very often discover at an early age how pleasant it can be to caress their own sex organs while girls usually take longer to find this out, which explains why girls who begin to masturbate often do so after some sexual experience.

It Is Quite Harmless

Researchers are agreed that masturbation is harmless and cannot lead to either mental or physical sickness. Neither, as some people believe, can it deform the sex organs nor prematurely exhaust them. The old myth that a man produces only a certain amount of semen in his life and therefore runs the risk of using up the supply unless he is careful has been shown to be nonsense. Similarly, there is absolutely no truth in the suggestion that you may later become impotent or frigid because you masturbate too much, though feelings of guilt about masturbation may mean that you experience such difficulties when you begin to have sex. But masturbation is not itself responsible for these problems. Some people blame masturbation because they feel tired or depressed or cannot keep up with their friends during sporting activities, but this is merely an exaggeration of ordinary experience following orgasm, when one may feel tired for about half an hour and need to gather one's strength again in the same way as one might after any demanding physical activity (a hundred-yard sprint, for example). If you feel tired and depressed for any longer than this interval then there must be other reasons—just as masturbation cannot affect your sporting performance unless you masturbate just before you are about to take part.

Although masturbation is harmless—just as not masturbating is harmless—some very shy and self-contained people may find great consolation in it and use it as a replacement for the emotional and sexual contacts that they find it difficult to establish. Especially when you are a little older and masturbation has become a habit, you may have difficulty breaking out of your isolation. Similarly, some people may continue to masturbate when they are married, using it to provide comfort and as a substitute every time any sexual difficulties arise, instead of tackling the problem together with their partner. In such cases it is not, however, masturbation itself that is at fault, but the way in which it is used.

On the other hand, there may be situations in which it is advisable to masturbate even if you do not usually do so. Here I am thinking of those situations in which a boy is making such desperate efforts to abstain that he becomes intolerant toward any friends he suspects of doing what he is not "allowed" to. There are also occasions when a girl is not satisfied by a sexual relationship because the boy has not discovered the right way to caress her and cannot ask her because she does not know either. If she learns to masturbate she can impart her knowledge to him, for the greater pleasure of both of them.

How People Masturbate

Boys usually masturbate by stroking or rubbing the penis or only the head of the penis rhythmically backward and forward between two fingers or in the hollow of the hand until orgasm is reached and the semen comes. Often this is done in such a way that the foreskin slides up and down over the head of the penis unless the foreskin is too short for this technique. Girls masturbate by rubbing the clitoris or the surrounding area rhythmically with one or more fingers until sexual climax is achieved. For both sexes it varies as to whether they take a firm hold or are more careful and whether they prefer fast or slow movements—though usually the faster and firmer the movements the nearer one is to orgasm.

Some girls may have a series of orgasms at short intervals without their sexual excitement decreasing noticeably between them, whereas boys who have just had an orgasm are rarely able to achieve another immediately afterward.

The realization that the technique may vary from person to person may be important when one first enters a sexual relationship. It is essential not to stick to one particular technique that one may have read about in a book but to make time to ask whether what one is doing is really what one's partner wants.

Variations in Masturbation and Masturbation Fantasies

There is nothing particularly unusual in using aids to increase pleasure during masturbation. Boys may use all kinds of objects as vagina substitutes. Or they may like to take their clothes off, sometimes looking at themselves in a mirror. Girls may do comparable things but, as far as is known, they are not as experimentally minded as boys. Both sexes may masturbate under running water in a shower or may use mechanical aids such as electric massagers.

Masturbation is often accompanied by sexual fantasies. Thus for certain people such fantasies will tend to repeat themselves, though they vary a great deal from person to person. Some may have realistic fantasies, based on some incident from real life that they have merely been prevented from satisfyingly concluding at the time, whereas others imagine more unrealistic situations. Some people may occasionally stimulate their fantasies with pornographic magazines. Masturbation fantasies are quite common and usually harmless, though, as we have mentioned earlier, there are those shy and solitary people who, apart from vivid masturbation fantasies, have a strong tendency to comforting but unrealistic daydreams. If you notice that you are doing this it is advisable to have a word with your doctor, a psychiatrist, or some other understanding person, before the tendency to slip from reality into the world of fantasy becomes too powerful.

Communal Masturbation

More than half of all men have at some time during their teens or early twenties taken part in communal masturbation with other boys or young men. This consists of either masturbating each other or taking part in masturbation at the same time. There may be competitions about who, for example, can squirt his semen the furthest, who can "toss himself off" the fastest, or who can achieve a climax most often, together with many other variations. The possibilities are endless.

Girls may also have experience of communal masturbation, though this is not nearly so common as with boys.

There is no reason to believe that you are abnormal because you participate in such activities, and no need to fear that you may more easily become homosexual because you have allowed yourself to be masturbated by someone else or have yourself masturbated another person. Homosexuality does not depend on your sexual activities during puberty.

Communal masturbation is a normal way of expressing your sexual impulses when you are young, and the sense of contact and fellow feeling that may result in the group or between two partners can sometimes positively help sexual development. As soon as you have the opportunity to enter a more prolonged sexual relationship with a member of the opposite sex, the desire for communal masturbation will, as a rule, disappear of its own accord.

5. About Love and Being in Love

Before passing on to descriptions of the more technical and physiological aspects of sexual life, I would like to say something about the emotional requirements that make a sexual relationship between two people successful.

You may go to bed with someone for a variety of reasons: because you are infatuated, in love, curious, worried about being different, eager to please your partner, afraid of losing him or her, or just plain randy. And intercourse can be satisfying on a purely sensual level, regardless of the depth of feeling involved, so long as both partners reach the desired climax. Moral attitudes are irrelevant as a basis for judging the reasons for going to bed, still less for condemning them.

However, long experience has shown that when sexuality and emotions are totally separated, the sexual relationship may become less satisfactory for both partners.

But we need to be more precise about what kind of feelings are involved. You may feel great affection for your pets, your brothers and sisters, parents and friends. You may like playing with your dog though these feelings will have nothing to do with sex. The fact that you are capable, however, of feeling affection for other people and animals may provide a foundation on which to build a permanent loving relationship later in life.

Infatuation

Especially when you are young, there are other, fiercer, emotions involved in the attraction between two people. We talk about falling in love or infatuation, and a strong infatuation can be an indescribable, almost ecstatic experience. The whole personality is involved in a feeling that pierces you right through. If the other person is also in love with you, you become immeasurably happy and everyone can see it. You walk more freely, your eyes shine more brightly, you feel very cheerful. All your good qualities blaze up just to please the person you have chosen—and to be encouraged by your friends and parents (unless the latter become anxious instead). But the strange thing about infatuation is that, even though the feeling may take hold of you in a matter of minutes, it can be so powerful that you regard it as a stroke of destiny. This experience becomes linked to all your ideas about "the one and only," and you have the unshakable feeling that you know the other person right to the depths of his or her being.

Obviously a state that can spring up so quickly need not necessarily have very much to do with the object of one's infatuation. It is above all a mental process that is provoked and maintained by the person one is in love with. In fact one is blind to everything except the things that have engendered the infatuation. After a time the other person's true personality is bound to emerge, and if you then find that they have many traits of character that you don't much care for, your infatuation will disappear, leaving a sad feeling of emptiness—or giving way to irritation, possibly even hate. Infatuation is subject to the harsh truth of the old saying "easy come, easy go."

"I love you" is an expression we whisper when we are in love—well, we feel the words inside even if we don't have the courage to say them. But it becomes an empty cliché when our infatuation fades and we still cling to the expression, as if to prove to ourselves and our partner that there is still something left of the old passion.

Although it is possible to experience such feelings in childhood, the infatuations of puberty are usually such an overwhelming experience that people have clear memories of them for the rest of their lives.

A Few Words about Responsibility

One of the characteristics of puberty is that one's moods and emotions are very unstable. One day you feel on top of the world and full of self-confidence, the next you are down in the dumps, depressed, insecure, and bewildered. If you are in a good mood you have a great deal of affection to spare for those you care for. If not, you hate everybody.

You may be very impressionable and your friends' opinion (or what you think their opinion is) may have a great influence on the way you behave. You may let the advice of adults, however sensible, go in one ear and out the other. It is essential for one's personal development that one gains mental and physical experience oneself.

Meanwhile there are certain kinds of activities that are bound to affect the lives of others or have incalculable consequences for one's own future, so that it may be sensible to listen to an adult's advice to think seriously before one embarks on them. Sexual activities belong to this category.

Adolescent boys and girls are still on an unequal footing as regards sexual matters and this may take any number of years to change. Although both may form romantic attachments without bringing particular sexual desires to the relationship, boys very often find that when they first fall in love they also feel strong sexual needs, a compelling wish to see their loved one naked, to caress her skin, to go to bed with her. Most boys who have reached sexual maturity have experienced during masturbation the delight of orgasm and now feel a deep desire to reach a climax "in the right way." Meanwhile only a minority of girls will have experienced orgasm through masturbation, so that being in love is not so directly bound up with sexual desires. Most girls, however, like the feeling of being admired and the romantic attention and enjoy cuddling and kissing. Such embraces invariably excite boys sexually, giving them an erection and an increasing desire to fuck. If a boy hasn't already reached sexual climax during such embraces (for this may be all it takes) he may get smarting pains in the balls, especially if the cuddling lasts for any length of time.

When one has reached this stage, such situations can obviously end in intercourse even if many of the requirements for successful lovemaking are not fulfilled. If it is the first time for one or both partners it may be a great disappointment, however much in love they are. And if one hasn't used any form of contraception the following months may be a nightmare. Indeed, only about one half of young people use contraceptives when they first have intercourse, not having foreseen that their embraces would lead so far.

The notion of responsibility has been abused by an amazing number of parents and writers on sex instruction. But the expression is still a valid one, for there is no denying the fact that some feeling of responsibility for one's fellow beings is tied to a mature emotional life. And these feelings of responsibility are strongest toward those people one cares for most. One may feel justifiably disillusioned when one looks at the world and sees the lack of responsibility and respect for others' life and liberty, especially in political spheres. But you need not despair because the world is in a mess. Your hopes and your potential form part of the future and to make the world a better place you should concentrate on your own development. Feelings of responsibility are to be taken seriously and falling in love provides one of the first emotional battlegrounds in which responsibility for others can prove itself.

For boys this means taking into account the fact that only a minority of adolescent girls have the same unequivocal sexual desires as themselves and determining not to try to force a girl into a sexual relationship that she is not ready for. For girls who have decided beforehand that they do not want to go all the way, this means remembering that many boys have strong sexual needs that can be unnecessarily provoked by persistently kissing and cuddling. If a girl has excited a boy although she doesn't wish to go to bed with him, she can always help him to reach a climax.

It is also essential not to try directly or indirectly to force someone to do something he or she would rather not, even if it leads to disappointment for oneself. This could be called the most important aspect of responsibility and obviously also applies in nonsexual circumstances.

About Love

Young people who have been in love several times only to see their feelings fade often wonder how men and women can manage to live their whole lives together. And of course there are those who can't—so they divorce, which is reasonable enough. Some of the couples who carry on living together may not actually care for one another very much but stick together because it's the thing to do or for practical reasons, possibly out of consideration for the children. There may also be other, even stranger reasons why two people continue a discordant marriage rather than live alone. If one's own parents are divorced or one suffers from having to listen to their continual squabbles, one may well begin to doubt whether love between two people can really exist.

On the other hand there are those, especially young girls, who place too much faith in the descriptions of love to be found in magazines and other forms of entertainment. Apparently, according to these romanticized accounts, one only has to marry him in order to live happily ever after.

One may imagine that one is experiencing love when one is infatuated. And this is not entirely wide of the mark since one may feel some of the basic aspects of love: warmth, optimism, interdependence, passion. And some infatuations last and mature into love.

This kind of development demands a great deal of emotional maturity, perserverance, and a will to contribute. One should never give up hope, though unless one can grow out of egoistic feelings, intolerance, and vulnerability, love has little chance of developing. These are some of the reasons why so many marriages do not work.

It takes time to build a fruitful and loving relationship, and though being in love can help to make it successful, this is not essential. There must be continual interaction between the two partners, a willingness to learn each other's qualities, peculiarities, and even defects, and to accept them, while continuing to smooth away the rough edges in oneself. One must work together to establish and maintain a home and to achieve the difficult task of creating a good environment in which to bring up children. One makes friends together and takes pleasure in each other's company. At every step of the way there may be difficulties, some of them so great that they assume the qualities of a marital crisis. Some people may give up at this point and extricate themselves. But overcoming such difficulties contributes to the slow growth of maturity, both for each partner separately and together. A relationship in which the partners have been able to develop tolerance, loyalty, cooperation, and equality never becomes boring, as some people think. Indeed one's interest in the other person is made more acute because a person who has these qualities will continue to look outward for the rest of his life.

Sex is important when you are really in love. Firstly, because it becomes a link in the great chain we call life, and secondly, because it should be a permanent ingredient of love and companionship and a means of reconciliation in those crises that even genuinely warm love relationships almost unavoidably run into.

A Few Words about Communes

Recently, many young people have banded together in communes. In some cases they have done so in protest against the narrow-minded attitudes of established society that conceives of the role of the sexes as based first and foremost on the concept of a family unit within the framework of marriage.

Some people have also had the vague idea that

anyone living in such a commune should also be more liberated sexually, so that it is no longer necessary to stick to one partner and one can have sex with whomever one wishes. But it is not always easy to separate the emotions and sexuality, and it may be wishful thinking to think that one can, because even in a commune people experience love, infatuation, resentment, and jealousy.

Communal living may well offer a new outlook for the future provided one accepts that most humans are first and foremost, one might almost say instinctively, pairing animals, who may well change partners several times in the course of their lives but who can only direct their strongest feelings toward one other at a time. (Some people do find it possible to create more stable three- or four-sided relationships, which may mean that we are veering toward an expansion of our emotional potential at some time in the distant future.)

About the Following Chapters

The next five chapters describe the various elements that help create a successful relationship between two people on a purely sexual level.

As we have said, it is quite possible to go to bed with each other and enjoy it without having great affection for one another. But infatuation and love are the strongest foundations on which to build a sexual relationship.

Sex can be the most pleasurable instrument of the feelings, and the sex organs are naturally the most essential tools of sex. We have already seen what the sex organs look like and how they function, but we need to know a great deal more about what they can do in order to enjoy each other fully. Although the art of love has been part of the education of young people in some cultures, it has hitherto been regarded in Western society as too risky to describe such techniques to young people as part of sex instruction. They might stimulate curiosity and excite sexual desires to such an extent that the uncritical would hop straight into bed with each other.

It is now known that this belief, which is still maintained by some people, is founded on sheer superstition, since there are completely different factors involved.

During puberty, when by far the majority have not yet tried to have sex, one may often entertain total misconceptions about sexual matters. This leads to one's first intercourse taking place in an atmosphere of such insecurity and anxiety that it may easily be disappointing, just as a boy may be so nervous that he does not put on a condom even though he has one in his pocket.

In fact the purely technical aspects of the art of love are so simple that anyone can learn them with a little practice. If many people do find difficulties, this is due not only to ignorance but more to mistaken ideas about modesty and lack of trust between the partners. If one doesn't dare express one's sexual desires to one's partner, sex may soon become a miserable business. But in such cases, there may also be something wrong with the emotional aspects of the relationship, since love and affection ought to overcome the kind of secrecy that destroys sexual pleasure.

6. The Senses and Foreplay

Humans seem to be made to make love. They have feelings, imagination, memory; they have lips, tongues, and hands; they have eyes, ears, a nose, and sex organs; and they have warm rooms in winter. And unlike other animals, humans have a sexual instinct that functions all year round, with small variations.

Sight

The appearance of the other person is an important erotic stimulus. Not special clothes, because fashions change as the wind blows, but their "vibrations," their way of moving, coloring, and body. We are not all equally beautiful, but, although society has a particular ideal of beauty, there is no need to despair, as tastes and likings differ and the person who is in love will find his or her partner the loveliest being on the earth.

In a sexual situation, the sight of a naked body can add considerably to each partner's awareness of the other, their feelings of closeness and excitement. So part of the experience can be lost if one of them modestly turns out the light.

Some people find it particularly stimulating on occasions if both partners keep some of their clothes on during intercourse or dress up in special garments.

Smell

For many animals, dogs for example, smell is an all-determining factor in the reproduction of the species. When in heat the bitch gives out a strong-smelling secretion from the genitals that can attract the male dog from a considerable distance. Once this smell is artifically removed by chemical means, some dogs will be hardly interested in mounting the bitch however seductively she behaves.

The human sense of smell is not nearly as well developed as that of dogs, though our body smell is just as strong. Even so, our appreciation of each other is incredibly affected by smell. Without noticing it and without even knowing it, we divide the people around us into those who have a strongly scented smell, those with a more neutral smell, and those who smell nasty.

Bad breath can really scare away the people around you—a fact that toothpaste advertisements outrival each other in demonstrating. Just changing the kind of toothpaste you use is not the important thing; the reasons are more complicated than that (see page 132).

Clean sweat can smell good and may be an erotic stimulant, but stale sweat gives off a rancid smell because certain bacteria can live off sweat and replace it with their own waste products. Daily washing will keep your skin clean enough, but if you do not find it sufficiently effective, you will find further advice on page 139.

As we have described earlier, the membranes of our sex organs secrete a waxy secretion of which the smell is, I suppose, counted as an erotic stimulus. The obsession of our hygienic era with dirt and the intimate connection between the sex organs and the excreta of the urethra and the anus have resulted in widespread aversion to sexual smells also.

Obviously the sex organs must be washed, preferably daily, for bacteria are also found in this waxy substance and can soon break the wax down into evil-smelling components. However, some people may find extra pleasure in not washing immediately before intercourse—they like people to smell human too.

Hearing

We can also receive erotic stimuli through the ear. Some people enjoy lovemaking to the accompaniment of music—the movements of intercourse are directed by the rhythms. Other people find mechanically produced sounds distracting, a subversive influence.

The amorous voice of the partner can be exciting in itself, though some people also like hearing dirty words—or saying them.

As intercourse progresses many lovers become increasingly disposed to utter groaning or whimpering noises. These are a wordless confirmation of pleasure and thus have a stimulatory effect on the other person.

Quite often the vagina makes "farting" noises during intercourse, especially if the penis is drawn right out with each backward pull. This is because all air is expelled from the vagina when the penis is pushed back in so that as the penis is withdrawn the air is sucked back into the vagina and sets the lubricated membranes vibrating as it passes along the walls. This sound is quite natural and nothing to be embarrassed about, just as there is no need to worry if the vagina makes slurping noises, which are merely indications that it is well moist. Otherwise one can always try another position; this will often make any noises disappear.

Touch

Certain areas of the body are more sensitive than others. Many people, though not everybody, are excited by being tickled, for example, on the nape of the neck, in the ears, on the lips, on the palms of the hands, around the navel, and along the vertebrae. Women's nipples are very delicate to the touch and stand erect when caressed, though often the man may be just as excited by fondling a woman's breasts as she is by his doing so.

The most powerful sensations are produced by touching the sex organs and the area around them. The most sensitive part of the woman is the clitoris, and of the man the head of the penis.

The excitement of feeling another person's body against one's own is usually an ingredient of every sexual situation. Indeed, it has such a thrilling effect on some people that even when they are separated from their partner's body by clothes they can reach a climax just by dancing together and pressing themselves against each other.

The Kiss

The members of some primitive societies never kiss, they rub noses instead. For us a kiss is felt to be essential as a form of expression, though some individual people shrink from "love kisses."

But a kiss is many different things. It may be the dry kiss we give to parents, aunts, and so on, or a form of greeting between friends. An erotic kiss is something completely different. The first one may be fumbling and unsure, an attempt to imitate what you have seen in old films—a dry, protracted, lip to lip kiss. Gradually you learn to part your lips and let your tongue play with the tongue and teeth of the other person. It can be a beautiful, exciting experience and stimulates the production of saliva, so that you feel as if you are "drinking from each other." Here the taste of the other person is very important. Bad breath or a nasty taste in the mouth may ruin everything.

It is not unusual for young people to collect kisses and even hold competitions to see who can manage to kiss the most people at a party, perhaps, or by a given time. You may try competing over who can go on kissing for the longest time.

In an erotic situation you will also want to kiss and be kissed on other parts of the body, and those places we have described as being the most sensitive to the touch will obviously be equally susceptible to kisses, licking, and sucking. There are also many people who like nibbling each other, though this requires a certain amount of caution, especially around the sex organs.

Foreplay

By erotic foreplay we mean loveplay that takes place before intercourse.

Foreplay actually includes the whole atmosphere in which intercourse occurs; and for a girl, especially, it is important to feel secure, secure with the man, certain that the time is right and that there is no danger of being disturbed, and confident that she is protected against pregnancy.

During actual foreplay, then, lovers caress and kiss each other in the most sexually impressionable places. Young men and women become excited very quickly, but most women require more time and gentle stimulation to reach the same degree of excitement as the man.

All types of petting (see next chapter) can be included under the heading of foreplay. Indeed, petting and foreplay are technically speaking the same thing except that with petting you are continuing foreplay right up to the point of climax.

7. Petting

Petting is an American expression which comes from the verb "to pet," meaning to caress. But petting means more than just caressing, it is a concept that covers the kind of loveplay in which everything except actual intercourse is allowed. Whether you go as far as intercourse or not is something you must decide for yourself, but first and foremost you should try to avoid an *unwanted pregnancy*. However, there are young girls who have another reason for just petting, and that is to preserve their virginity for their wedding night.

In any relationship in which there is a strong element of eroticism, there will be degrees of petting involved, right from the first kiss to the most advanced foreplay. But once we have established that petting can be satisfying by itself we will have isolated the "process" we intend to examine in more detail in this chapter.

As we have said, people often react irrationally in sexual situations. Petting, however, if it is cultivated in order to avoid pregnancy, would seem to be highly rational. You want to make love but you do not want to have children and you are not certain of the effectiveness of the available means of contraception. You know deep down that if you did become pregnant you would want an abortion. So taking all the consequences into consideration, you "make do" with petting.

Besides, petting can have an added advantage over intercourse. You learn to recognize each other's sexual responses more quickly because you have to pay more attention to your partner. Just as in intercourse, the object of petting is the satisfaction of both partners. In fact, this can be achieved more easily with petting because the man can concentrate more directly on the sensitive parts of the woman if he wishes to, thus enabling the woman to obtain pleasure from their contact.

Although you are being sensible, that is not always enough, since petting can only be satisfactory if you show initiative and independence. The process demands that both partners talk intimately to each other and have the courage to show the other partner which line of action they most desire him or her to take.

The Techniques of Petting

Petting is not always something you have decided to do, but may develop gradually. You kiss, caress, and squeeze each other, eventually find your way under each other's clothes, become less inhibited and more bold, more or less undress each other, and begin to search with your hands for the other person's sex organs.

One day one of you has an orgasm and for a while you may continue petting just to achieve this again, but gradually—or so one hopes—a wish develops for the other person to achieve a climax too.

The Woman

Lack of experience in the woman means in most cases that the man has greater difficulty satisfying a girl than the other way around. If she has never masturbated to orgasm she cannot tell him exactly what he should do. The man should continue to experiment with guidance from the woman. Sometimes, however, the problem may prove insoluble, in which case it may help if she learns to masturbate and conveys her experiences to him.

As we have said, the clitoris is the most sensitive part of the woman. The exact position of it can be seen in the illustration on page 20. The man can try rubbing it gently, making sure that it is well moistened. If not, he can take some of the lubricating fluid from the vagina or possibly use spit.

If she likes what he is doing and can't suggest anything better, then he is on the right track. As he carries on she will gradually become more and more excited. Then something unexpected may happen: it feels as if part of the clitoris is disappearing under your finger. The man may take this incorrectly as a sign that she has come, and if she does not know what an orgasm is, she may even resign herself to the removal of his finger without complaining. In this way, the whole business may prove one-sided and unsatisfactory for her because her body has become excited and she is not able to find any release.

What happens is that when a woman reaches a certain degree of sexual excitement, the clitoris is drawn back and up under a fold of skin. It is a sign that she is well on the way, but not there yet. If the man allows his finger to slide up in the same direction as the clitoris he will be able to feel it under the fold of skin and continue in the same way he began. If he cannot find it properly, then she should help him. If she is still satisfied with the way he is rubbing her, then it will not be long before she reaches orgasm.

At the approach of, and immediately after, orgasm the clitoris may become extremely hypersensitive and the woman may find it virtually insupportable to be touched there. But this does not necessarily mean that she has come as much as she wants to. As we have said, some women can have several orgasms one after another, and it would be a shame to cheat her of the rest, especially as the second or third orgasm in the series is quite often the most powerful and satisfying.

So, after stopping for a little while, the man can try gently rubbing her again, though not if she says that she is satisfied and does not want any more.

Some women, however, cannot stand direct contact on the clitoris—they find it downright painful. If this is the case, the man can try pursuing a less direct course of action by putting a couple of fingers around the clitoris and moving them rhythmically, for example, or pushing the mons veneris (the mound with hair on it) backward and forward a bit with his fingers or the flat of his hand. There are also several other possibilities, and since the man cannot guess beforehand what is going to be best for the woman, *she* should control the direction, pressure, and speed of what he does. It sounds very simple but can be really difficult before you "hit on the right tune," so to speak.

One of the reasons why we have discussed satisfying the woman first is that it is most gratifying for both partners if she reaches orgasm before he does (unless, of course, you are aiming at simultaneous orgasm, in which case see below). For after the man has reached orgasm, and he tends to come more quickly, he may sometimes lose his sexual appetite to such an extent that he is no longer interested in satisfying the woman. He may not even have the energy. But the woman's sexual excitement diminishes more slowly, and even after several orgasms she usually still has the ardor and energy to carry on and help him to a climax.

Satisfaction in Men

When the time comes for her to satisfy him, she can do so either passively or actively. If it is the first time, many girls prefer to be passive, or, more accurately, they haven't the courage to be active. But passivity on the part of the girl can make things difficult for a young man, especially if he is a bit shy. Since he must not use the vagina, he has the problem of finding a substitute. He may be able to reach a climax between her thighs, but there is a risk here that if he is lying too far up some of the semen *may* find its way into the vagina and result in fertilization.

The most common practice is for the man to find a vagina substitute in the hollow of her hand or hands and by himself making the movements to reach a climax there. Of course he may also use her armpit, for example, or sit astride her, putting his penis between her breasts and gripping the breasts together around it to make a "sheath." Some kind of lubricant will always make this more comfortable.

If she is more active, the woman can masturbate him in the hollow of her hand or hands by bringing them up and down over the penis. But in this case, it is important that *he* should show *her* the correct way to do it, and that *she* should ask *him*.

Variations

If both partners are satisfied by petting, they are usually content to continue doing what they enjoy for a fair while. But they may have sneaking feelings of dissatisfaction, rooted in the fact that they really want to go to bed with one another. If the girl can take the Pill, then there is no reason not to carry petting through to intercourse, since the Pill when correctly used affords complete protection against pregnancy. If her doctor will not prescribe the Pill for her, she can try asking another doctor, since attitudes to contraception vary a good deal. Otherwise the couple may continue petting so that it becomes more satisfying.

You can start by licking each other's sex organs until you reach orgasm. For this, the man should kneel forwards between the spread legs of the woman and find the clitoris with his tongue. He then makes the same movements with his tongue as he would with his fingers until she reaches orgasm. Every now and again he can vary this by licking her on the labia and a little way up into the vagina, but the main pressure should fall on or around the clitoris. He can also give her even greater pleasure by putting a finger up into the vagina while he is licking her (there is generally room to do this even if she still has her virginity) and then, when she comes, he will be able to notice how the walls of the vagina contract rhythmically around his finger.

She can satisfy him by kneeling forwards between his legs in the same way and taking the head of the penis in her mouth. She can support the penis in her hand, pull the foreskin right back and then begin moving her lips up and down over the top. At the same time, she can make sucking motions and rub with her tongue.

Many girls will pull their heads away when the semen comes, but this kind of staving-off reaction is usually unsatisfying for him unless she finishes him off with her hand. Quite a few men have a more or less hidden desire for their partner to take the semen in their mouths. Many women, even experienced ones, have a deeply rooted objection to this variation, whereas others are quite content with it. Admittedly it seldom has a sexually exciting effect on the woman.

The woman must be careful not to bite the penis, since her teeth can easily tear holes in the membrane. Instead she can suck the underneath of the head of the penis and rub it with her tongue until he has an orgasm, since this is the most sensitive area.

If you intend to reach orgasm at the same time, or almost the same time, you can try lying in such a way that the man has his head in the woman's crotch and she has his penis in her mouth. This position is called sixty-nine because the two numbers, when put side by side, look like two people making love in this way. If you can work out how to do it, it is probably the most satisfying form of petting, though when the man is much taller than the woman, or the other way around, you may find it difficult for both of you to reach each other's sex organs at the same time.

You must also remember that the woman should *never* lie underneath the man as she may be choked by the semen if he is very violent (this has been known to happen).

The possibilities we have discussed here should give a young couple a good indication of how they can have a pleasant, varied, and exciting sexual relationship even though actual intercourse is "not on." This is not to say that all the possibilities have been exhausted, and it must be stressed that no variations, however peculiar, that are used by a loving couple to excite and satisfy each other can be called "perverted" (that is, sexually sick or abnormal) as long as they are agreed about what they are doing and not worried by anything. Take anal eroticism, for example. It is not unusual for one or both of you to put a finger into the anus in certain sexual positions, for example, sixty-nine. Many people find it surprisingly pleasurable.

It is less common for the anus to be used as a vagina substitute. If the woman strains her anal sphincter she finds it painful (and it can be hard to relax again). If the man is too violent he may cause hemorrhoids (varicose veins at the opening of the anus) and tear the membrane. If you are determined to try, the man should smear himself well with vaseline or a lubricating cream and take the whole thing very cautiously.

Is Petting Unhealthy?

No researches have concluded that petting is unhealthy, but it is always important to be clear about your motives for particular forms of behavior. If, for example, you wish to keep your virginity for your wedding night, that is in itself a powerful motive for continuing to pet until you are married. But you might also ask yourself why your virginity is *so* important. After all it is only the minority of young men who want their brides to be "pure."

It seems rather hypocritical of a girl to want to make love and at the same time to protect the evidence of her virginity. Why should intercourse be any more immoral than petting? That is why girls who do this are called "technical virgins."

The desire to avoid pregnancy is very right and proper. If one cannot or will not take the Pill, then petting is the only known safe method of satisfying each other and, if both partners are satisfied with this, there is no reason why one should not carry on with it for years.

The chances of becoming pregnant during menstruation—especially if the man also uses a condom —are so microscopic that there is no need to hold back through fear of pregnancy while you have your period. But this is somewhat messy.

But in situations where the time, the opportunity and the desire have taken you unawares and you have no contraceptive device, and assuming that you do not want to have each other's children, then petting is the only reasonable way to satisfy each other.

8.   Intercourse

The most intimate association between man and
woman is generally called intercourse or coitus. Expressions in common use for having intercourse are
to make love, to fuck, to go to bed together, to have
an affair, but of course there are innumerable other
slang names for the same thing.

Intercourse is preceded by a more or less lengthy
period of foreplay. At intercourse, the man's erect
penis is put into the woman's vagina, generally by
her guiding him in with one hand while she holds the
labia apart with the other. One or both partners then
move their pelvis and possibly the whole body as well
in such a way that the penis slides backward and
forward in the vagina. After a certain amount of
time, which may vary from a few minutes and in
some situations up to several hours, these movements create an increasing sensation of pleasure that
may spread from the sex organs to the whole body.
The muscles become tense, respiration more violent,
and the movements often quicker and deeper, until
intercourse culminates in one or both partners
reaching a climax, that is, orgasm.

Positions

Intercourse can be accomplished in many different
positions. The most common is that in which the
woman lies on her back with her legs apart and

slightly bent at the hips and knees, while the man lies above her with his legs together, supporting himself on his knees and elbows so as not to be too heavy. This position can be varied. The woman, for example, can try bending her hips further towards her, possibly by putting her legs up over the man's shoulders while he gets up onto his hands. It can sometimes help, especially if you are lying on something soft, to support her bottom with pillows or cushions so that the clitoris is in a more impressionable position.

Alternatively the man can lie on his back while the woman sits astride him with one leg on each side of his body. She can then lie down over him and stretch out her legs more or less. In this position the woman has more freedom of movement and can thus determine where, what and how fast the actions should be. This position is most popular in those parts of the world where love has traditionally been a pleasurable activity and the art of love has been developed.

You can also "mate" like animals. The woman kneels forward on her stomach with a pillow under her pelvis or lies on her side with her legs bent up from the hips so that the man can enter the vagina from behind. Even women who find it easy to reach orgasm, however, will find it difficult to do so in this position because the clitoris is virtually untouched— unless one of the partners stimulates it with his or her fingers at the same time.

In addition, intercourse can be carried out while the woman sits on the man's lap, while both partners are standing, and so on. What we said about petting also applies here: that as long as there is complete agreement and no embarrassment about what you are doing, your sexual experiments will never become "perverted," however peculiar.

It is worth emphasizing, however, that women who do not find it easy to achieve orgasm during intercourse will very seldom be interested in experimenting. The man will often be extremely excited by new variations, making the woman justifiably afraid that he will reach a climax too early, so that she does not get anything out of it. She may have had great difficulty in learning how to achieve orgasm in a particular position and will understandably prefer that position for some time, until she gradually becomes more sure of her own responses.

Afterplay

Afterplay is a poor word for the intimate atmosphere and the gentle caresses that may follow warm and satisfying lovemaking. Especially when two people are in love, they feel a desire to lay themselves open, chat with each other, and look for encouragement and comfort in each other.

In more established relationships when the partners know each other well, or in relationships where there are less feelings involved, there may be less need to devote time to afterplay and the couple may fall asleep instead.

Communal Sex

This expression is used to describe sexual activities in which more than two people participate and make love either alternately or at the same time. Such relationships are usually three- or four-sided, as, for example, with two women and one man, two men and one woman, or two men and two women. They occur spontaneously in the majority of cases, or as sexual experiments, in which case less account is taken of emotions.

64

9. Sexual Response and Orgasm

As we have now stated several times, certain influences on the sexual organs result in an increased state of sexual tension that can be relieved after a certain period of time in orgasm. So it is time to describe what actually happens and what a man and a woman feel.

Orgasm is also called satisfaction, sexual release, sexual climax, or just climax, and to have an orgasm can be called "to come," "to give," "to shoot," to be satisfied or gratified, and to achieve a climax—we have already used several of these expressions.

Sexual Excitement in Women

As women become sexually aroused a number of physiological changes take place in their breasts, sex organs, and skin.

The nipples become erect, the breasts swell, and, as excitement increases, the brown area around the nipples swells up so that it can sometimes look as if the nipples have suddenly lost their firmness.

Excitement in the genitals causes the vagina to produce lubricating fluid that then leaks down to moisten the entrance. The clitoris and the labia minora swell and change color and the labia majora open outward to make room for the penis to enter. In addition, a flush very often spreads over the front of the body.

As sexual tension rises, the clitoris is drawn back and up under the fold of skin. The inner two thirds of the vagina expand while the outer third swells. At this stage the man may be able to feel these changes in the vagina as a firm tightening around the penis.

Orgasm in Women

Orgasm entails a series of brief, rhythmical contractions, or "spasms," in that part of the vagina that has swollen up. In addition, there will be similar contractions in the womb and possibly in the floor of the pelvis and the anal sphincter.

After orgasm the changed areas of the body revert to normal quite quickly, though at different rates. Thus the swollen, brown area around the nipples will decrease again more quickly than the actual nipples, so that the nipples may suddenly look as though they are beginning to stand erect again.

The woman's own experience of these physical changes will depend chiefly on whether the orgasm is the result of masturbation or brought about by intercourse.

During masturbation (either being petted or on one's own) consciousness of pleasure is concentrated in the clitoris. The constant, uniformly rhythmical rubbing provokes increasingly intense sensations of enjoyment in and around the clitoris, and these gradually spread up into the vagina proper. Eventually these sensations are mingled with a powerful feeling of warmth that travels from the pelvis over the whole body. When the outer third of the vagina swells, it will feel as if a contraction were taking place there. Sensual pleasure will have now reached its highest peak and will be concentrated into a pulsating, throbbing sensation in the clitoris and the vagina, corresponding to the stage at which the outer part of the vagina is rhythmically contracted. This pulsating feeling may spread to the whole of the body and finally seem as though it has synchronized with the heartbeat. At the height of orgasm many women also feel an enjoyable tingling in their tensed muscles and even have the sensation that their brain has become temporarily disconnected.

As we have mentioned earlier, in many women one orgasm can succeed another without any drop in the level of excitement between the two. After a single orgasm however, or a series of several, an agreeable relaxation and general decrease in tension will run through the body and muscles and a drowsy peace will fall over the woman.

For many women orgasm during intercourse will, broadly speaking, take the same course, except that the sensation in the clitoris is seldom as intense as during masturbation. This is because the clitoris is not exposed to such direct pressure during intercourse as it is during other forms of release.

Other women experience orgasm during intercourse as an apparently deeper sensation and they may have a strong desire to feel the penis standing right up in the end of the vagina. In fact, reaching a climax may depend on this, in spite of the fact that there are few actual nerve endings in the wall of the vagina itself.

Even so, the chief reason for the release of sexual tension in orgasm is the indirect stimulation of the clitoris, produced by the compression together of the pubic bones and the pushing on the labia as the penis is drawn between them.

It is therefore no more superior to be able to have a deep vaginal orgasm than to have a clitoral orgasm, as they are two aspects of the same thing. Physiologically there is no difference between the two sorts of climax.

All that we have said so far has been about physical responses and sensations. In sex this is never the whole story, and even the most promiscuous and least involved man or woman will have emotional involvement at some level with every partner. Even masturbation almost always involves certain fantasies. When a young man masturbates, however "clinically" he may start—perhaps merely to relieve his tension or frustration, which may have been completely nonsexual in origin—as masturbation develops toward orgasm he will generally develop fantasies of some kind or another. A similar thing, perhaps less physically orientated, occurs whenever a girl masturbates.

There is nothing standardized or uniform about the emotions men and women experience during sex. The ideal relationship of tenderness, love, sharing, and giving, with a multitude of other positive emotional qualities on either side, is achieved remarkably frequently, but sex between two people who do not even like one another cannot in itself create this relationship. Many other powerful emotions may be released by sex, such as jealousy, revenge, domination, and the desire to hurt or to be hurt—all are normal at intercourse and many young men and women have been deeply frightened to experience such strong and unpleasant feelings released within themselves by sex; occasionally the experience can be so traumatic that a period of revulsion with or without a period of actual impotence can result. Most young men and women find it very difficult to talk about such things—even to their lovers or, perhaps, particularly to their lovers—and suffer much guilt in the belief that they are abnormally disturbed by sex.

Sexual Excitement in Men

When the man is sexually stimulated, the spongy tissue of the penis is filled with blood that is pumped in through a "sluice" so that it cannot flow back. This means that the penis becomes stiff, firm, and much larger, until finally it stands erect away from the body, tilted slightly upwards and possibly very slightly to one side. This is called an erection, or a "hard-on." When the man is extremely excited a couple of drops of clear, lubricating fluid may also run out of the urethra.

Gradually, as sexual tension progresses, the balls will also swell and both the scrotum and the balls will be drawn up toward the floor of the pelvis, where they will remain during climax. If the man is sexually aroused for some time *without* having an orgasm, he may experience some pain in the balls because they have become so large and strained.

Just as in women, a flush may appear over the front of the body of an excited man.

Many young girls are scared the first time they see a naked man with an erection. While kissing or hugging close to a boy they may have noticed that something in his trousers grew big and hard and felt strangely disturbing when he pressed against them. All the same, though, they hadn't imagined it would look *so* enormous.

Western society seems to be officially ashamed of this response in a man that is, after all, so common and natural. Our museums are full of statues of naked people, but not one of the male figures show an erection even when they are portrayed in erotic situations. Where we are ashamed, however, other cultures have been proud, and in many places the erect penis has been worshipped as a fertility symbol. You will find that the art of the world abounds in examples of this worship, for instance, Indian temple art.

Orgasm in Men

During orgasm a number of muscular contractions take place that finally result in the prepared semen being squirted out through the opening of the urethra (the "eye" in the head of the penis). These contractions rhythmically divide the semen into small portions. This stage corresponds to the point in a woman's orgasm when the swollen walls of the vagina are rhythmically drawn together. The man's anal sphincter may also move.

In contrast to many women, by far the majority of men can achieve only one orgasm at a time; that is to say, it will normally take one-half to several hours before you can get another erection and reach a new climax. The number of times a young man can reach orgasm during the space of six hours, for example, varies a great deal with the individual. It may be anything between one and five to six times. So as long as you can manage it once there is no need to worry.

Just like women, men can experience the physiological aspects of orgasm in different ways, but for them the difference lies more in the strength and intensity of the sensation than in its point of departure. The greater the amount of semen, the longer and more powerful the climax will be—another reason why the first orgasm in one night, for example, is usually the best.

During both masturbation and intercourse the regular pressure on the penis will result in increasing physical pleasure, a feeling that is most strongly concentrated in the head of the penis but also spreads into the floor of the pelvis and, in some men, up over the whole body. The man also sometimes experiences a feeling of warmth.

Just before climax he will notice that the semen is on its way and at a certain point he will find it impossible to control his responses. The semen is going to be released whether he wants it or not. The height of orgasm is reached immediately before and during the first muscular contractions that push forward the semen. And, just as in women, orgasm may be accompanied by a luxurious tension in the muscles and followed by relaxation and a dozy feeling of comfort.

A Few More Words about Orgasm

Although both male and female orgasm presupposes some physical stimulation of the sex organs in by far the majority of cases, the following examples will show that this kind of influence is not always necessary.

When asleep, both sexes may have such erotic dreams that they reach orgasm—you may find yourself waking up in the middle of climax. If you have a great many erotic dreams, they may be interpreted as a sign that you do not get the necessary degree of satisfaction for your sexual needs when you are awake.

It is also possible for certain men and women to reach a sexual climax solely by listening to particularly stimulating music, reading suggestive or exciting books, or seeing similar pictures or films. Moreover, some women may reach orgasm solely by stimulation of the nipples, while exhibitionists (see pages 121–122) can sometimes achieve a climax just by exposing their sex organs. Perhaps the strangest thing is that men can ejaculate involuntarily if they are suddenly overcome by powerful feelings of worry or panic (during some kind of disaster, for example).

All these things just go to show how complicated the orgasmic reaction really is. It *can* be produced quite "mechanically," but just as often it will embrace wide areas of your mental life.

The Older Generation

Those sexual reactions that are purely physiological tend to somewhat decrease in sensitivity and intensity with age. Such changes in sexual needs and capabilities vary greatly with the individual and are especially susceptible to mental factors.

To generalize, one can say that the more intensely one cultivates the sexual side of life, the better one will preserve one's sexual vitality through the years. This applies to both men and women.

Some young people are unhappy at the thought that their parents and even grandparents still have an active sex life. In my opinion, one should be glad that such a rich source of sexual and emotional experience can be drawn on throughout one's life.

10. Difficulties in Intercourse

Not only humans, but also animals, can have difficulties with intercourse. The sight of a tiny dog trying persistently, but quite unsuccessfully, to mate with a large bitch is both sad and funny.

The comic side of such difficulties doesn't occur to you when you find yourself beset by some insoluble sexual problem. And yet it may often be just the serious, self-centered lack of humor with which you tackle the situation that makes it seem so overwhelmingly important.

Pains during Intercourse

It is natural for a girl to have some pain with her first intercourse—though this is not the rule. The pain is caused by the breaking of the hymen and to a lesser extent by the stretching of the vagina. In some girls the hymen is very thick and tough. If, at the same time, the entrance to the vagina is small, intercourse cannot take place at all. If the entrance is larger, there may be room for the penis to enter, but any movements it makes in the vagina will cause pain. It is hard for the girl if the man forces his way in without any consideration for her, much better if he stops trying and they carry on petting.

Pains during intercourse may also be due to the fact that the girl is so nervous that she starts getting cramp in the vagina. This condition, appropriately called vaginism, can completely close the entrance to the vagina, so that the man cannot push his way in at all. In some very rare cases it may be necessary for the girl to have her hymen broken "medically" by a doctor.

If this is the case, pressing on regardless will not help, but only make matters worse. Instead one should try and find out why the girl has become nervous in the first place. There may be many reasons. Perhaps she is afraid of becoming pregnant, or worried that she may be disturbed or discovered. If it is the first time she may be scared because the stiff penis is so big and formidable or just alarmed at the idea of being really grown-up. What both partners must realize is that with vaginal cramps the body is spelling out what the girl herself dare not or cannot say, namely, that she either cannot or will not accept sex fully until her problems have been satisfactorily solved.

Dryness of the vagina is one of the things that can be disagreeable, and possibly painful, especially during the initial movements of intercourse. This dryness is very often due to overimpatience on the part of the young man. It takes time to prepare if you want to make love well. But it may also be because the girl is nervous, so you should try and find out why.

If the girl uses a diaphragm, the jelly that comes with it will act as a lubricant. If, on the other hand, you are using a dry condom you may find it helps to smear a little lubricating or spermicidal jelly on it. If neither of these is at hand, then spit, though not very suitable, is better than nothing. Never use vaseline—petroleum jelly destroys rubber.

Over and above these causes of pain during intercourse, some women have slight aches in the womb, especially during the days before menstruation. Very deep movements during intercourse can thus cause pain in the abdomen when the penis hits the cervix. This usually happens in connection with positions in which the vagina is foreshortened, for example, the position in which the woman lies on her back with her legs drawn right back or the position in which the man enters from behind while she is kneeling forward.

This can be remedied by lengthening the vagina, which will happen if, for example, you lie in the ordinary position (the woman on her back, the man on top) and the woman keeps her legs stretched more or less straight during the movements. If she lies or sits on the man she can determine how deep the penis should enter herself. It is also possible for the man to try and penetrate less deeply and violently, but this is often more difficult, especially just before ejaculation.

Aches in the womb *may* also of course be due to illness (see pages 138–139).

Sexual Coldness or Frigidity

People talk a bit disparagingly, and misguidedly, about a woman being frigid or cold if she has never got anything out of a sexual relationship or, more specifically, if she has never had an orgasm during intercourse—even though this is almost never due to any lack of sexual impulse.

Quite often a "cold" girl feels abnormal and worries if her condition continues. And this worry may strengthen the mechanisms causing her "frigidity", if the causes are latent in her and not the fault of her partner. In this way she can slip into a vicious circle that may be difficult to break.

When you begin to go to bed with each other, both

of you must adapt yourselves to the fact that you are moving into an area of experience that is unique and different from any other kind of personal contact, because you can enter so quickly into each other's lives—both physically and mentally. That nature has made it so is marvelous and wonderful, but also full of pitfalls and difficulties, because as humans we are laboring under a mass of sexual prejudices influenced by the culture in which we live.

Against this background it is hardly surprising that we can make an awful mess of lovemaking, especially when we are young and everything is so new and untried, and there is no unprejudiced and experienced adult we can go to for guidance.

So it is not unusual for it to take several years for a young woman to lose her frigidity.

Knowing that frigidity in the young is more usual than unusual may help. However, you should try and find out if the causes lie with the young man or with the girl. Is he too impatient? Does he come too quickly? Has she something against him that she does not dare admit? Perhaps she doesn't even care for him very much but just fucks with him because all their friends do and she doesn't want to be left out? But the reason can also lie in herself. Is she afraid of becoming pregnant? Nervous of moral condemnation from her parents? Afraid that she won't be good enough? Or, as we suggested above, just afraid of being grown-up?

Obviously it can be very difficult to unravel the threads, but if you make an honest attempt together, you will find that the contact between you has become richer and more fruitful. This in itself may relax the kind of frigidity that is psychologically conditioned.

Frigidity can also be due to awkwardness and lack

of technical expertise. First and foremost, you must make sure that intercourse takes place in some quiet, undisturbed place and that you have plenty of time, preferably a couple of hours. If you cannot supply *this*, it is naïve to expect the girl to get anything out of the experience.

When you have arranged to be in peace and quiet, then it is important that both partners should allow themselves enough time for actual foreplay. If the young man becomes very excited during foreplay and knows from previous experience that it will take very few movements during intercourse to make him come, it is probably most satisfying for the girl if he continues the foreplay until she has reached a climax (see Petting) before he starts on actual intercourse.

Usually it is easier for the girl to reach orgasm in those positions in which the clitoris comes under the maximum pressure. For many couples the most suitable position will be the most usual, where the woman lies on her back with the man on top, or the other way round. He should then try to bring as much pressure as possible to bear on the area surrounding the clitoris, using the region round his pubic bone. The movements should not be too expansive, but uniform, continuous, and uninterrupted. The shorter the movements, the more constantly the clitoral region will be stimulated and the easier it will be for him to hold back his orgasm until she comes. He will interrupt her excitement if he suddenly decides to try a new position or withdraws to put on a condom. So it is sensible for *this* reason also to put on the condom before intercourse. (See also page 93, where there is a reference to the contraceptive reasons for doing this.)

She can also do something herself to draw in the

labia minora and move the clitoris by training the muscles in the pelvic floor to make "pincer" movements (as is recommended after giving birth) and then try to make use of these movements during intercourse. She will discover that concentrating on these movements will increase her sensitivity around the entrance to the vagina.

To reach climax at the same time is a real art, so you should not be disappointed if it doesn't happen. If the man comes first he can satisfy the woman afterward as we have described on pages 55–56 and 58. If she comes first she will usually find it very enjoyable to continue until he is finished too.

As you gradually get to know each other better, he will become more familiar with her responses immediately before orgasm and will be able to wait right until the last minute before loosening all the restraint he has imposed on himself. She might possibly help by either telling him or making some sign or sound at the right moment.

If he can satisfy her by masturbation, but not through intercourse, however good his intentions or his lasting power, then you can try a combination of the two in which he has his penis in the vagina while either he or she is stimulating the clitoris with a finger.

If he cannot satisfy her either by masturbation, intercourse, or a combination of the two, then she may perhaps try to learn to masturbate so that she can convey her experiences to him. Psychological problems on her part, possibly together with a certain selfishness in him, may make the whole thing so impossible that you give up trying. If you are still very fond of one another in spite of your difficulties, then you might try seeking advice, either separately or together, from a doctor, a psychiatrist, a psychologist or your local family planning clinic.

This is not to say that loving relationships should develop into a desperate struggle for orgasm. There is a tendency these days to regard orgasm as a sort of status symbol that no woman can afford to be without. But the partners' feelings for each other are much more important, and provided the woman feels mentally satisfied by intercourse, she will find the relationship so gratifying that it will be equally valid.

The important thing is to be honest with yourself and to try and achieve whatever form of physical and emotional satisfaction you have most need of at the time.

Premature Ejaculation

So much has been said about the girl's problems that one might have gained the impression that any trouble is always her fault and has nothing to do with the man. But in fact it can very often be lack of ability on his part that is responsible for their contact being unsatisfactory for her.

By premature ejaculation we mean exactly what we say, that orgasm comes and the semen is released long before it is intended. If the young man is intensely excited sexually, ejaculation may occur before he enters the vagina or immediately after he has done so.

Obviously the first time you have intercourse you may be excited and nervous in just this way and it can happen very easily. If there are long gaps between sexual encounters then intercourse may again feel so new and exciting that it is impossible for the man to control himself.

And it does not matter terribly if the first orgasm

comes too early as most young men will be potent again after half an hour or two hours and the intervening time can be used for foreplay.

If it only takes a few coital movements to bring you to a second orgasm, then this will create even greater problems. But the only thing you can do in that case is to try a third time and once again make the best possible use of the interval that must elapse before the man is potent again. At some time or other the man will probably be lucky enough to stay in the woman long enough for her to come with him. Unfortunately this remedy will be of any use only to people who are sure of an undisturbed room for long periods at a time. If you only have a few hours, or even less, you will have to deal with the matter in a slightly more practical way: the man can try masturbating before his encounter with the woman. This will ensure that his sexual excitement and sensitivity is not so great. If you are not using a condom, you might try putting one on, as this will also reduce sensitivity.

An American doctor has reported on a young man who trained himself to avoid premature ejaculation by masturbating—or letting the woman masturbate him—until the point just before the semen came (this can be seen quite distinctly) and then ceasing to apply any kind of pressure so that the orgasm was not achieved. He then waited for about fifteen minutes before doing the same thing again, repeating this process altogether about three to four times. This treatment was then carried out for three to four days and led to the desired degree of self-control. In W. H. Masters and V. E. Johnson's *Human Sexual Inadequacy* (1970) this method is not considered very effective. Instead there is a description of a new method of achieving total control over the moment of ejaculation. It would be too complicated to explain this method in detail here, but it may be helpful to borrow the book from the library and study the contents yourself if the methods described above have proved ineffective.

If none of the methods described achieve satisfactory results, a psychiatrist may be able to help either by prescribing special tablets or by helping the man over the psychological problems that are usually at the root of the trouble.

There used to be people who supported circumcision as a remedy for premature ejaculation, but it has been seen to have no effect.

Absence of Ejaculation

Some boys cannot reach orgasm however hard they try. This may be due to nerves or to the fact that they do not really care very much for the girl. However, you will usually be able to reach orgasm and ejaculation by masturbating. If you can't even do this, then it is probably because you are too young and not sufficiently mature sexually. Both women and men have difficulty in reaching orgasm after drinking alcohol, since alcohol reduces sensitivity in the sex organs.

Some men will, moreover, experience these kinds of difficulties when they use a condom. So the girl must obviously make sure she gets a diaphragm or start taking the Pill.

Impotence

Impotence is an inability to carry intercourse through to orgasm. Thus the condition described as absence of ejaculation is a kind of impotence, though usually the word impotence is used to mean an inability to achieve an erection in those situations where it is called for.

Many young men become more or less impotent the first time they go to bed with a girl. This is due to a strong sense of anticipation and to overexcitement. It is as if you are taking an examination and your mind goes blank, even though you knew the answers perfectly well before you sat down.

But impotence is also a very common occurrence in later sexual relationships, especially when you are going to bed with a girl with whom you are not entirely relaxed. It is likely that the more you care for her the more easily you will find yourself impotent, since her opinion of you matters a great deal. Obviously the less interested you are in somebody the less vulnerable you are to their opinions.

The source of a great deal of impotence lies in the fact that people are more prone to boasting and exaggeration about their sex lives—about the size of their penis, their ability to make love, or their potency— than about any other area of experience. If you are credulous and swallow all your friends' stories, you may begin to feel inferior, even if you are a keen boaster yourself. So when you are about to go to bed with a girl, your feelings of inferiority may intrude, especially if you know that she has made love with other people and is in a position to make comparisons.

A young man who has pretended to his friends of both sexes that he is an unbeatable lover and who then finds himself justifiably doubtful about his sexual superiority may well be abandoned by the potency he worships. He will feel wounded and humiliated by the situation, almost irreparably so.

Any kind of impotence can become a vicious circle, because once you have had the experience of being impotent the worry that the same thing will happen again is enough to ensure that it does. Thus some men may become impotent over fairly long periods of time, though they always regain their potency.

Many young people have their first experience of impotence after drinking alcohol, and this may be completely unexpected because alcohol tends to increase sexual desire and attraction and lower inhibitions.

Impotence can also accur *after* a man has achieved an erection—if he is having difficulty putting on a condom, for example. He may then mistakenly think the fault lies with the condom and that it is not a suitable form of contraception for him. Or, whether he has a condom or not, it may suddenly feel as though he has lost contact with the vagina in the middle of intercourse. This is because the vagina widens as the woman becomes progressively excited, but the man may begin to doubt whether he is erect at all and these doubts will make him lose his erection.

How should you tackle the problem of being impotent? First and foremost by not taking it, and oneself, too seriously: it is not a disaster. Probably, without knowing it, you have a lot of fellow sufferers. Instead, try talking to your friends about the problem; admit your imperfections instead of boasting. They will probably take their courage in both hands and confess their own minor weaknesses. You may even find that by taking the inititative in this rather surprising way you have created a friendlier and healthier atmosphere in the class or at work.

When you find yourself impotent in a sexual situation, you should talk to the girl in the same way and tell her that it is quite a usual occurrence that will adjust itself again, possibly not today but another time. Once you have said this, you should not lie and wait for an erection or allow her to feel at fault, but talk about other things.

The woman, for her part, should accept the situation—and if she did not know it before, then she now knows that it is something that occurs to many young men. There are women who feel hurt by the man's impotence because they take it as a sign that he does not care for them or desire them enough. As we have said, nothing could be more mistaken. In fact the reason may well be that he cares too much.

The worst thing the woman can do is to show impatience, let alone contempt. This will naturally have the effect of bringing his impotence home to him. He cannot get an erection just by wanting to do so—the desire and will to achieve an erection may be so all-absorbing that it just won't happen.

If you have lost your erection after putting on a condom, there will obviously be a strong temptation to pull it off and take a chance without it. But it is more sensible to treat this kind of impotence in the same way as any other, and lie and wait, talking with the girl, with the condom on.

If you have lost your erection during actual intercourse, then you should calmly begin again. You might possibly satisfy her by masturbation first, if she was about to come when you broke off. This will also relieve whatever feelings of guilt or incompetence the interruption has provoked in you and make it easier for you to overcome your impotence.

There can, however, be more permanent forms of impotence, due either to great psychological opposition between the lovers or to some deep-rooted aspect of the young man's adolescence and his whole relationship with his mother. Only a psychiatrist will be able to help unravel the threads of this kind of problem.

Very few impotent men are homosexual. And if they are, the prospect of intercourse with a woman will provoke not only impotence but also an unqualified disgust at the woman's sex organs.

Tightness of the Foreskin

Tightness of the foreskin (or phimosis) can sometimes also cause difficulties in intercourse. This is dealt with more fully on pages 134–135.

Adjusting to Each Other

Even if you like each other very much and get on very well together, great conflict may arise when the sexual urge is stronger in one than in the other. Especially if you live together, get married, or just have opportunities to be alone with each other a great deal, such a discrepancy may well make life less idyllic.

In most cases it will be the young man's sexual urges that are stronger, though later in life the situation may change, so that the woman feels greater desire.

If it is the man's urges that are stronger, it may be a burden for the woman, even if their relationship is a good one, to be in a state of sexual preparation one to several times a day. She may find that sexual contact requires more preliminaries, may want to work up to a certain frame of mind. If he is very demanding sexually he may even risk her dislike. In this situation it is possible to relieve him of some of the surplus sexuality without her being overtaxed. This can be done by masturbation either by the girl or by himself, though how often should obviously be determined by the individual. And one should be able to talk freely about the problem. Of course he can always go to other women, as long as she accepts this. But, even when she is not particularly narrow-minded, infidelity is a difficult thing, especially when it is one-sided. You may easily find yourselves slipping away from each other or creating hopeless conflicts.

On the other hand, the woman's sexual urge may be stronger than the man's. This, in fact, makes the problem even greater because a powerful sexual impulse in a woman is unacceptable to many men who either disparage her or become afraid of her (or disparage her because they are afraid).

If a woman demands and insists on a greater sexual performance than the man either needs or is capable of achieving, he may well begin to dislike her, especially if he has had a conventional upbringing. And he may sometimes become impotent out of fear that he will not be adequate when he actually does want to go to bed with her.

A possible solution here, also, is that she should begin to masturbate or that he should satisfy her by masturbation when he does not wish to have intercourse with her.

Otherwise she has the alternative of finding herself a lover, though because of our prejudices it is often even more difficult for a man to accept infidelity in a woman than the other way round. This applies especially in those situations where she is looking outside the relationship because his sexual drives are insufficient.

Can One Make Love during Menstruation?

Some men do not care for the idea of the woman bleeding during intercourse. A few find it totally distasteful. But on the whole, women have an exaggerated idea of men's aversion. Thus in many lasting, warm sexual relationships, the initial disinclination to make love during menstruation may disappear altogether in time.

If the woman is bleeding a great deal, as she may during the first day of menstruation, she can always insert a diaphragm before intercourse. This will stem the flow during actual intercourse, though she must remember to take the diaphragm out immediately after intercourse. Otherwise there may be a risk of incurring an abdominal infection. Obviously, however, when a diaphragm is being used as a means of contraception it should not be removed for at least six hours after intercourse.

The woman need have no anxiety that intercourse during menstruation can harm her vagina or womb and there is always the advantage that there is very little possibility of fertilization during her period.

11. Contraception

In modern society our sex lives are inextricably bound to the question of how we are going to avoid unwanted children.

As soon as sexual maturity is reached, with production of semen in boys and menstruation in girls, it is possible for fertilization to take place during intercourse.

Superstitions

Some people think that so long as one partner is under a certain age—fifteen, for example—then the girl cannot become pregnant. But since sexual maturity can be reached much earlier, the concept of such a natural form of contraception is completely false. Sometimes a girl begins to be sexually active before she is fully fertile (because she is very young, she may not ovulate every month), and she may leap to the conclusion that she *can't* become pregnant. However, a girl can become pregnant any time after menstruation has begun, regardless of her age or past luck. The same applies to the belief that you cannot become pregnant while you are breast-feeding a child. You can; even if you still haven't had your first period after birth. The risk is simply less great than it would otherwise be.

There is also a widespread misunderstanding that if a woman remains "cold" during intercourse, that is, does not reach orgasm, then she is sure not to become pregnant. Equally mistaken is the belief that the position in which the woman lies on top with the man underneath affords certain special protection. Finally, there are some people who think that a woman cannot become pregnant if she has been diagnosed by a doctor as having a retroverted womb (a womb tilted backward) or if her abdomen has been exposed to X-rays as part of some examination.

All these and similar notions are pure superstition and are responsible for the birth of many unwanted children every year.

BAD METHODS OF CONTRACEPTION

Coitus Interruptus

This is the method in which the man pulls his penis out of the vagina immediately before the ejaculation. This method has been know for thousands of years and used by many, including Onan, as described in Genesis (see page 31). But it has many drawbacks.

First of all, it is very unsafe. Male lubrication may contain active sperm cells that will be left in the vagina when the penis first enters it. Furthermore, before the final, large portion of semen comes—and so that you can't notice it—a small amount of lubrication also containing active sperm cells may be released. Besides, the semen is very often ejaculated onto the woman's outer sex organs, and since the sperm cells are mobile they may penetrate the vagina.

Not only is it an unsafe method, it is also very unsatisfying, because intercourse is broken off at the very time when it is by far the best. In terms of feeling, it is probably most shattering for the woman who does not manage to reach orgasm, but it isn't much fun for the man either. Altogether, any opportunity for feeling a sense of union is destroyed, and for many couples this may be as enriching a part of their relationship as the whole act. There will also be an increased risk of fertilization if any further intercourse is engaged in, even if the man washes his penis and urinates in between.

So if the man promises to be really careful and means by this promise that he is going to break off intercourse, the girl should not feel completely safe —since it is in the nature of the act that he may not be able to keep his promise however much he wants to.

If you find yourself in a sexual situation and have no protective device with you—and this can happen to everyone—it is much safer to satisfy each other by petting than to use coitus interruptus, which is unsatisfactory and very risky.

"The Safe Period" (Rhythm Method)

Theoretically and in practice a woman should be *most* liable to become pregnant at the moment of ovulation, that is, about fourteen days before the start of the next period. Since sperm can live for some days—possibly even longer—inside the female sex organs, you have to reckon on the most *unsafe* period being about eighteen to ten days before the first day of the next menstruation, supposing that menstruation is regular. Inversely the *safest* period should fall during menstruation itself, five to six days before and a couple of days after.

Moreover, ovulation is indicated by a small increase in body temperature of about 0.2° to 0.4° Farenheit, about 0.5° Centigrade. So if you take your temperature every morning at the same time before you get out of bed, you will be able to fix this point in time exactly.

Although this is the only form of birth control officially allowed by the Catholic Church at the moment, I do not recommend the safe-period method. The time of ovulation can vary slightly from month to month and may be influenced by many external factors, especially when you are young. Besides, now and then you may either want or have the opportunity to make love during just the eight days or so when you aren't allowed to, so that you become irritable with each other or break the ban and take a chance. Finally, it would seem that there are some women for whom there simply is no "safe period," and the only way you can find out if you are one is by getting pregnant.

Spermicidal Suppositories

These are hard waxy lumps sold in drugstores without a prescription. They are meant to be inserted into the vagina at least fifteen minutes before intercourse (so they have time to melt), but not more than thirty minutes before. *If* your timing and self-control are right on, and *if* the thing melts, it will form a temporary chemical barrier that kills sperm before they enter the cervix. Contraceptive suppositories are probably better than nothing, but just barely.

Spermicidal Creams and Foams

These can be bought without a doctor's prescription too. They are used during intercourse (inserted not more than one-half hour before) and a fresh application is needed for each ejaculation. Foam comes in aerosol cans; creams and jellies come in tubes; and there are special applicators to help you get the right amount into the vagina up next to the cervix. Although better than nothing in an emergency, none of these is really safe when used alone; however, used in combination with a condom, a diaphragm, or an I.U.D. they increase safety and may give some protection from V.D.

METHODS THAT DON'T WORK AT ALL

Douches

For decades people have thought, or hoped, that washing out the vagina immediately after intercourse could prevent fertilization. But the truth is that more than enough sperm make it through the cervix, where they are entirely out of reach, before you ever make it to the bathroom. Douching with fancy solutions from Coca-Cola to organic raspberry will not make the slightest difference, except perhaps to give you a rash.

Homemade Condoms, Feminine "Hygiene" Products

Caught unawares, some people try to fashion makeshift condoms from sandwich bags or plastic wrap. These aren't nearly strong enough to do the job. Others, using their imaginations, think that products like vaginal "hygiene" sprays or suppositories may provide some protection. They will not, unless clearly labeled "for contraception," and even then they are not a good method.

RELIABLE MEANS OF PROTECTION

The Condom (Protective, French Letter, Rubber)

The condom is a rubber sheath that is rolled down over the stiff penis like a fingerstall. Before you put it on, you can unroll the condom just a little to see which way it should be rolled on. Then you draw the foreskin back and slowly roll the condom down over the penis. If you rush it, you risk getting some of the rubber you have already rolled on stuck into rings—then you have to roll it back until it has come unstuck and lies smooth.

While you are putting it on, try to make sure that no air gets in between the condom and the penis, since air bubbles have been known to cause the rubber to split. If the condom has a teat, or sperm reservoir, twist the teat round a couple of times before you put the condom on. You must also be careful not to tear holes in the rubber with your fingernails.

You should put on your condom before actual intercourse, for the reasons we have listed above under Coitus Interruptus, otherwise safety is diminished. Besides, you may also find it difficult to put on the condom once the penis has become moist at the beginning of intercourse. In such cases you will find it easiest to dry yourself thoroughly before rolling the condom on.

You can find both dry and lubricated condoms on the market. The latter are a bit more expensive and more difficult to put on but are recommended in those cases where the girl is suffering from dryness of the vagina. Since there is usually a reason why dryness of the vagina exists, your relationship will improve if you try and find out the cause rather than assume that everything is fine as long as you have a lubricated condom. If you would really rather have some supplementary form of lubrication over and above the vaginal fluid, it is cheaper to smear a little contraceptive jelly (which you can buy at any drugstore) on the outside of the condom when you have rolled it on. Do *not* use vaseline or other petroleum jelly, since it will destroy the rubber.

When intercourse is over and the semen has been released into the condom, it can easily slip off if you keep on moving or wait until the penis is limp again before you withdraw. So the most sensible thing is to withdraw immediately after orgasm, holding the condom in place with a couple of fingers while you do so.

Some people think that it is safer to put on two condoms at once. It isn't, on the contrary, the two condoms may easily rub each other to pieces during the movements of intercourse.

When the used condom has been drawn off, the penis will be covered in a wet layer of semen that both partners may get on their fingers if love play is continued. The semen can be conveyed from the fingers to the woman's outer sex organs and from there the sperm cells may be able to travel into the vagina. So if you are going to continue love play, it is advisable for the man to wash his penis and his hands thoroughly—he might even urinate as well—so that the remains of the semen are washed away from the urethra.

Before you embark on intercourse again, you should have a new condom on. If you haven't any more with you, then you will have to make do with petting. Or you could wash the used condom thoroughly on both sides, dry it and inflate it to the size of a milk-bottle. You should then hold the in-

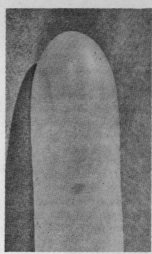

Above Left: a condom with teat. *Right:* a condom without teat. *Below:* two samples of wrapped condoms.

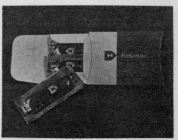

flated condom up to a strong light and examine it carefully for tears, finally powdering it with talcum powder or something similar. Then the condom can be rolled up and will be ready to use again. Most good condoms will stand up to this treatment, but don't try it too often.

Condoms can be bought in drugstores and in family planning clinics. They are also available in vending machines in men's rooms at gas stations and elsewhere. They cost from ten cents to about thirty cents apiece. All condoms made in the United States have been subjected to the same tests, so they are equally effective; the extra cost may be for reservoir tips, lubrication, an especially thin membrane for extra sensitivity, or even your choice of festive colors. The most important thing to remember is that condoms have a safe shelf life of about a year, and those lying about in vending machines may be much older, or they may have been exposed to heat or cold, which makes them deteriorate faster. Drugstore or family planning clinic supplies will be safest and may be cheaper as well.

A condom does not give you complete protection even when it is correctly used, because it can tear or perish. If you want to increase safety you can use it in combination with spermicidal suppositories, creams, and sprays, or with a diaphragm. A combination of this kind is particularly suitable during the eight days of possible ovulation (see page 90) if you do not want to risk having a child on any account.

Although a condom can be bought so discreetly nowadays that even the shiest person should be able to overcome his embarrassment, statistics show that many young people fuck without any kind of contraceptive. There are several reasons for this and one of them is that young men do not make the effort to get themselves a packet of condoms.

If it became common practice for young boys of fourteen or fifteen onward to buy themselves a few packets and practice using them during masturbation, they would be able to avoid many unwanted pregnancies later on. If you are masturbating in any case, you might just as well learn how to put on a condom properly so that you will be prepared when it matters.

Furthermore, it would be practical if both girls and boys made it a habit always to have one or two condoms with them for protection against conception and V.D. Condoms in individual foil packets are avilable for this; as long as you don't unwrap them they will last in your pocket or purse for up to a year.

Diaphragm (Pessary)

The diaphragm is a rubber "bowl" with a flexible metal ring round the edge. It is always used *with* some kind of spermicidal cream. The cream is spread around the outer edge and then a blob left in the middle on both sides of the rubber. The diaphragm is then inserted into the vagina as shown and described in the illustration, though it can also be put in place with a specially made applicator.

Used correctly a diaphragm affords the same amount of protection against pregnancy as a condom. It is not 100 percent safe. If you want to be absolutely sure, it may be advisable to use both a diaphragm and a condom during the eight or so especially risky days between two periods.

If you have intercourse several times during the course of one evening, you should use a syringe applicator and insert a new blob of spermicidal jelly or

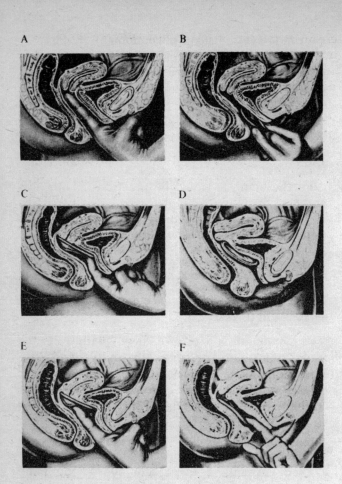

A. The first time you insert a diaphragm, it is wise to locate the cervix first so that you know how far up it actually is. **B.** The diaphragm is now squeezed together and ready to be inserted. **C.** Push the diaphragm right to the end of the vagina so that the top edge sits in the hollow behind the cervix. Then push the nearest edge forward and upward with your fingers so that the diaphragm is held in position by the back of the pubic bone. **D.** This shows the dia-

cream at the top of the vagina before each of the male partner's ejaculations.

Before inserting a diaphragm, the bladder should be empty. Then you should take the diaphragm and smear the contraceptive cream on it. Next, you stand with one foot on a chair (or squat), squeeze the diaphragm together between your fingers, and you are ready to push it up into the vagina.

The diaphragm should not be taken out until at least six hours after the last time you had intercourse. It should then be washed, dried, and held up to the light while you draw the rubber slightly taut toward the metal ring to make sure that it is not torn in any way; then it should be powdered with talcum. It is not necessary to give yourself a douche either before or after you remove a diaphragm.

Unlike condoms, which will fit any man, a diaphragm can only be given to a girl after her vagina has been measured. You can be measured by a private gynecologist, at a family planning clinic, or at one of the private clinics specially set up for young people. At a family planning clinic all consultation is cheap and the actual diaphragm may cost you less than elsewhere. Private consultations cost from $10

phragm incorrectly placed. This can happen if you do not push the diaphragm right up behind the cervix, but under it instead. As you can see, the cervix is then unprotected, allowing the semen access to the mouth of the womb. *E.* After you have inserted the diaphragm, check with a finger that you can feel the cervix through the soft rubber dome of the diaphragm. *F.* Take the diaphram out—at least six hours after you last had intercourse—by putting your finger up along the front wall of the vagina and grasping hold of the front edge of the diaphragm. Then pull it out slowly and carefully.

to $35, depending on where you go; this price will probably include the diaphragm itself, or you may be given a prescription for one. You can buy cream or jelly at the drugstore without a prescription for about $2 a tube. (Be sure to get an applicator as well.)

Since the vagina grows during puberty and afterward, it is wise to have your measurements checked every six months or so. Similarly, new measurements must be taken after giving birth or undergoing an abortion, or after gaining or losing ten pounds or more.

Since the rubber rots slightly after a time, you should always change your diaphragm once a year. You can do this without a prescription at most drugstores as long as you know which number to ask for, or take the old one with you.

The age at which a girl may be fitted for a diaphragm without her parents' consent varies from state to state and even from town to town. In most places girls of eighteen will have little trouble; if you are younger than that you can call Planned Parenthood for service or for a referral to a private doctor sympathetic to minors. In any case, before a doctor can take the measurements the girl must be "deflowered," which means that the hymen has been broken and the entrance to the vagina more or less unblocked. For most girls this means that they cannot get a diaphragm until they have had some experience of intercourse—and this is undeniably a disadvantage.

One advantage of the diaphragm over the condom is that you can insert it several hours before you expect to have intercourse and, as a rule, neither partner will notice it is there during intercourse. So if you are going to a party where you think you may be drinking, it is safer to have put the diaphragm in your vagina than in your handbag. It isn't the slightest bit silly to be as careful as this and there's nothing degrading about going home again *without* having needed to make use of this kind of protection.

Intercourse often takes place spontaneously on such an occasion, when you are becoming sexually excited by dancing with someone or caressing him and at the same time your inhibitions and common sense are diminishing under the influence of alcohol.

The Intrauterine Device (I.U.D., the Coil, the Loop)

The I.U.D. is a small gadget made of plastic or of metal coated with plastic that is inserted in the uterus by a doctor. It probably prevents conception by altering the lining of the uterus so that a fertilized egg cannot implant itself in the womb. Its advantages are that it is with you all the time, has few dangerous

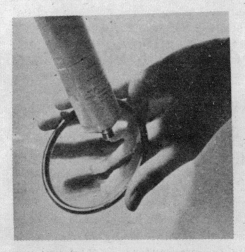

Contraceptive cream and diaphragm.

side effects, and is very effective, though not 100 percent. It does have some disadvantages: it causes cramps and heavy bleeding in some women and has to be taken out; some women expel the device without knowing it and become pregnant; a few women become pregnant even with the I.U.D. in place. Also, most doctors have been reluctant to insert an I.U.D. into a woman whose cervix has never been stretched by pregnancy or childbirth, but recently a smaller I.U.D. called the "Copper Seven" that can be used by most women has been placed on the market.

For those who can use it, the I.U.D. is an excellent method of contraception, particularly if a backup method such as condoms or foam is used during the days when the risk of pregnancy is greatest. When pregnancy does occur with an I.U.D. in place, the I.U.D. does not harm the fetus and will be delivered along with the baby if the pregnancy is not terminated.

The coil, showing the different shapes available.

A 100 Percent Sure Method

The Pill is the only method of contraception that affords complete protection against pregnancy *as long as you remember to take the pills according to the directions.* It works by preventing ovulation, which must take place before an egg can be fertilized.

Specialists have confirmed that a young girl can start taking the Pill without any serious risk as soon as her monthly periods have been regular for a couple of years. This actually means that a number of girls could begin doing so as early as fifteen to sixteen without any detriment to their development.

The Pill can be obtained from a doctor who, before issuing your prescription, should give you a thorough checkup to ensure that you are not suffering from any of those diseases that can be aggravated by the Pill (see page 106). It comes in monthly packs containing twenty, twenty-one, or twenty-two pills. When you first start taking the Pill, you take one the fifth day after the first day of your period regardless of whether you are still bleeding a bit. Then you take one pill every evening before you go to bed for the next twenty days or so, according to the number you have left in the pack. You stop taking them for six to seven days and then start on a new pack. During the interval you will have a period, which is often weaker and shorter than normal.

The Pill does *not* ensure against pregnancy during the first month you are taking it, so you must continue using some other contraceptive device.

If you have forgotten to take the Pill in the evening, you can catch up again the following morning. But if there is a gap of more than thirty-six hours between taking two pills there is a danger of ovulation taking place. So, if you have forgotten to take your pills for more than thirty-six hours, you should continue to take them until the pack is finished, but you will also have to protect yourself with some other form of contraception and then start with the next pack five days after you have begun your period in the usual way.

It can be quite difficult to remember to take a pill every evening. Have a good think about it and put the pack in some place where you are bound to "fall over it" every day, on your pillow, perhaps, or in your tooth mug. Obviously it is most difficult if you don't want your parents to know and have to hide the pack every time you take one.

You may find that you have forgotten to take the pills with you when you go away—for a weekend with friends, for example—and be tempted to borrow a couple from a girlfriend. But if you don't keep to the same brand for the entire twenty-one days you run the risk of ovulation taking place, because the different brand names contain different quantities of hormones. To be on the safe side, you should again use another form of contraception while continuing with the pills. The same applies if you have been suffering from vomiting and/or diarrhea, since you cannot be sure that the pill has remained in the system long enough to be absorbed.

The first month you take the Pill some of you may be bothered by nausea and feel generally unwell. These troubles usually disappear if you continue taking the Pill. If these symptoms are really nasty see your doctor, who can always prescribe another brand after your period. It may be a question of not being able to take the particular combination of hormones selected by one make, while

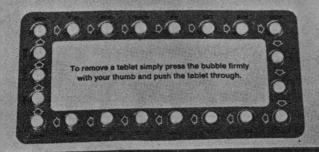

HOW TO USE NORINYL-1

This is all you have to do. On the 5th day of your period, take your first tablet and continue to take 1 tablet every day until your first 3-week pack is finished. Your protection starts from your very first tablet. Leave 7 clear days before starting the next 3-week pack. Now you have no more counting, just '3 weeks on, 1 week off'. Your period will come during the tablet-free week, which you can now note in advance on a calendar. Your protection continues during the week you are without tablets.

Take the tablets regularly at a set time such as before going to bed. If you miss a tablet, take it as soon as you remember and continue as before.

If your period comes early. If a full monthly period starts before all 21 tablets have been taken, stop the tablets, wait 5 days, and start all over again with a new pack. Do not worry about any slight spotting of blood between periods, and do not stop your tablets.

If your period does not come in a tablet-free week and you have taken all the tablets as directed, it does not mean that you are pregnant. Start your next course after 7 tablet-free days whether or not menstruation has occurred. If you miss more than one period, tell your doctor.

If anything unusual happens. Sometimes, slight discomfort occurs at first, such as a feeling of sickness. This will soon disappear and you can look forward to the comfort of painless periods and freedom from premenstrual stress. If you are in any doubt see your doctor.

To be taken under medical supervision.

To remove a tablet simply press the bubble firmly with your thumb and push the tablet through.

A packet of contraceptive pills.

another will give you no trouble at all.

Another side effect of the Pill is that you may put on a little weight. This may be particularly bothersome if you were plump in the first place. The increase in weight is chiefly due to the fact that the Pill causes the body to retain more liquid (as it does during pregnancy). Thus some people will combine the Pill with tablets intended to expel the liquid again. This is really going a bit far. You can keep your weight down without using artificial or dangerous means by keeping a watchful eye on your calorie intake.

Since the Pill is the most effective method of contraception available at the moment, you should give it a fair chance before you decide you can't live with any side effects you may feel. Remember that the vast majority of women experience no discomfort at all, and that the physical and emotional risks of pregnancy could be much more harmful than some temporary indisposition. But remember, too, that for the few who should not take the Pill it can be extremely dangerous. So you should never take the Pill unless it has been prescribed for you by a doctor. *Never* borrow pills from a friend. Conditions such as heart and kidney disease, high blood pressure, diabetes, epilepsy, migraine headaches, severe depression, and others can be seriously aggravated by the Pill, and you could have such a condition without knowing it. If you should have persistent serious side effects while on the Pill, report them to a doctor (and don't let him or her brush you off as a "nervous female").

Most doctors recommend that you go off the Pill periodically. Some feel that you should take a month off every six months, some feel you can stay on the Pill for three or four years, then stop for a while to let your normal body chemistry get back into gear (during which time you use some other kind of contraception).

Finally, it is possible that the Pill has an added advantage over every other kind of contraceptive. Menstrual troubles and pains may be reduced or disappear, you may get rid of spots and breasts which seem 'too small' will sometimes become a little larger. Similarly very thin women may find that they are getting a little more flesh on their bodies.

The Future

Scientific research continues to explore new forms of contraception, just as there are still attempts to improve the existing methods.

Thus, experiments are being carried out on new forms of "coil" in the hope of finding some design that offers complete protection, and work is in progress on a completely new type of Pill in which the hormone supposedly responsible for blood clots is replaced by a completely harmless but equally effective substance. It is also believed possible to produce a pill that will not prevent ovulation but will create an impenetrable mucous plug in the cervix, so that the sperm cells cannot reach the egg.

Still at the experimental stage, there have been attempts to give the contents of the Pill as an injection once a month, and there are even experiments underway on inserting the contents of the Pill under the skin in small "packages" that give the hormones off into the blood at such a slow rate that the contraceptive effect should last several years.

Some research, though not enough, has been done on a "Male Pill" that would prevent release of sperm into the semen. Others are working on temporary sterilization procedures in which tiny plastic clips are used to block the fallopian tubes in women or the sperm ducts in men. At the moment the most emphasis is being given to several procedures that are not really contraception, but "after the fact" fertility control. One is the "morning after" pill, which is available now but used only in emergencies such as rape. This is a massive dose of female hormone (estrogen), and almost always gives one a bad case of "morning sickness" that may last for days.

Perhaps more promising is a hormonelike substance called prostaglandin, which produces contractions of the uterus. At the moment, it tends to cause cramps and sometimes nausea, but if these effects can be overcome it could be used to make the uterus safely expel its contents at any time during pregnancy, from immediately after conception right up to full-term delivery.

A third technique currently being studied is called menses extraction, or mini-abortion. When the period is late, a plastic hand syringe is used to suck out the lining of the uterus. It is quite quick and safe and is done in a doctor's office with little or no anesthetic, before a test can even show if pregnancy has occurred. For all these reasons it is usually less upsetting and certainly less expensive than a regular abortion. However, most doctors feel there has not been enough long-range study of the technique, and others feel that morally it is the same as abortion, so it remains controversial.

12. Abortion or Birth

The First Signs of Pregnancy

If menstruation fails to take place or is very weak and lasts only a short time, possibly with the blood a more brownish color than usual, it may be a sign that you are pregnant. But you may have a late period or miss one altogether without necessarily being pregnant. Fear of pregnancy alone can disrupt the menstrual cycle.

Nausea, morning sickness, general malaise, and tiredness can be early signs of pregnancy, but may also be the outward expression of pregnancy fears. The only way to find out is to have a complete pregnancy test. If you are not pregnant you will save yourself a lot of needless worry, and if you are, the sooner you know it the better you will be able to decide and arrange exactly what you want to do about it.

A pregnancy test consists of two things: a urine test and a doctor's examination of your uterus. Neither one is enough by itself. After you miss your period you must wait two weeks; this is to allow a certain pregnancy hormone to become detectable in your urine and for certain changes in the size and color of your womb to become noticeable. Fourteen days after your period was due, make an appointment with a doctor. You can go to a private doctor if you can afford it; you can call the family planning clinic at a hospital or the Health Department for a referral; or you can go to Planned Parenthood for either the test itself or the name of a doctor who will treat you confidentially.

If the pregnancy test is positive, that means you are pregnant. Pregnancy is counted from the *first* day of your *last* period, not from conception, because nobody knows for sure when that was (even if you only had sex once all month, fertilization might have occurred days afterward). If you are very regular, and if your pregnancy is confirmed two weeks after you miss your period, you are considered six weeks pregnant.

What Is an Abortion?

By abortion we mean the termination of the pregnancy before the fetus is viable or capable of independent life. Practically speaking, the fetus must be under seven months old. A normal pregnancy lasts about nine months, though some births take place between the seventh and ninth month, in which case they are called premature births, since the baby has a good chance of survival.

Abortion can occur spontaneously if the womb cannot retain the fetus for some reason and expels it before time. Most spontaneous abortions, or miscarriages, take place during the first three months of pregnancy. The earlier they occur, the more difficult it becomes to tell them apart from a heavy period. It is therefore acknowledged that many spontaneous abortions take place without the women knowing they have been pregnant. If there is any reason to suppose that you have had a spontaneous abortion, it is sensible to go to a doctor, since it may be necessary to scrape the womb to remove the remains of the membrane surrounding the fetus and the placenta. This scraping, or curettage, takes place in a hospital and is carried out by a gynecologist, or specialist in women's diseases. About 10 percent of pregnancies end in this way.

An abortion can also be brought about by intervention in the womb. The operation may take one of several forms, depending on how far advanced the pregnancy is. From the eighth to the twelfth week of pregnancy a doctor can remove the contents of the womb manually with an instrument that he or she inserts into the womb through the cervix. The womb may be gently scraped out with a spoonlike "curette" (this procedure is called a "D&C"—dilation and curettage); or a vacuum curette may be used to suck out the contents of the womb.

Between twelve and sixteen weeks, there is no safe abortion method because the fetus has become quite large and the walls of the womb are stretched very thin. After sixteen weeks a different technique, called a saline abortion, is used. A doctor inserts a needle into the womb, removes some fluid from around the fetus (called amniotic fluid) and replaces it with salt solution. This brings on contractions of the uterus within forty-eight hours, and the fetus is expelled. Though statistically safer than carrying a baby to term, saline abortion is more dangerous than early abortion and often more traumatic, so it is important to arrange an abortion before the twelfth week of pregnancy whenever possible.

The Legal Status of Abortion

Until the nineteenth century, a woman's right to have an abortion before the baby "quickened" (moved) was taken for granted. When New York passed the first anti-abortion law in 1820, the reason was to protect women's lives, since surgery of any kind was then extremely dangerous. Later, more and more states passed similar laws, but by that time the Victorian era was in full swing. Anti-abortion laws helped to make illicit sex dangerous, which people thought a very good thing; besides, the laws kept the population growing, which people also thought a good thing. By the 1960s, however, a lot had changed. Surgery had improved to the point that a legal abortion was far less dangerous than carrying a baby to term. (In New York City in 1972 there were 29 maternal deaths for every 100,000 childbirths and only 3.5 per 100,000 legal abortions.) Attitudes about sex, women, and population growth had changed as well. States began to change their abortion laws, so that in some places you could have an abortion simply by claiming you were having a nervous breakdown, while in others you couldn't even if your life were endangered. In the meantime, illegal abortions were increasingly available to those who could afford them and knew how to go about it while thousands of poor, young, or ignorant women were maimed, made sterile, or killed by back-street criminal abortionists and by the most dangerous abortionists of all —themselves. Desperate women tried to end their pregnancies by douching with caustic solutions, swallowing strong drugs or poisons, or sticking sharp objects into their wombs, usually with disastrous results. Increasingly it became clear that laws against abortions did not prevent either illicit sex or abortion; they only made abortion difficult, discriminatory, and dangerous. By 1972 four states had made abortion legal "on request" at least up to the twelfth week of pregnancy, and in each place maternal death rates dropped dramatically, as did infant death rates (because mothers too old, young, or ill to have babies could choose not to) and out-of-wedlock birthrates.

In January 1973, in a landmark decision, the Supreme Court ruled that all the remaining laws against abortion violated the woman's right to privacy as guaranteed by the Fourteenth Amendment of the Constitution. The Court held that whatever medical or religious opinion may be, the fetus is not a person in terms of the Constitution. Specifically it stated that anyone may have an abortion before the twelfth week of pregnancy as long as it is performed by a doctor. For pregnancies between twelve and twenty-four weeks the states may make laws concerning medical practice—that is, they may require that an abortion be done in clinics or hospitals to protect the woman's safety—but they may not interfere with her decision. For pregnancies of seven months or more, when the fetus may be viable outside the mother's body, the states may prohibit abortions, but they still must be allowed to protect the life or health of the mother.

In some areas it may still be difficult to find a doctor willing to perform an abortion, since the law does not require any doctor to do so against his or her wishes. Also, in some areas it will be difficult to find a doctor willing to treat a minor without the consent of her parent or guardian. In such a case, a girl can call the nearest Planned Parenthood or Clergy Consultation Service for advice or referral. (See page 141.) But unless the Supreme Court's decision is overruled by passage of a Constitutional amendment (unfortunately this is always a possibility) it should never again be necessary for a woman in the United States to submit to the pain, danger, and humiliation of an illegal abortion, or to continue a pregnancy she doesn't want.

Is It Dangerous to Have an Abortion?

Whether the operation takes place in a hospital or not, there is always a certain risk involved. A certain number of deaths occur every year as the result of abortions, though they represent a very small percentage of the number of abortions carried out. It is worth pointing out that the risk involved in continuing the pregnancy is statistically far greater.

Complications may take the form of infection, which gives rise to high temperature, pains, or heavy bleeding. Such infections may result in sterility or an inability to have further children. If such complications occur while you are in hospital, then obviously immediate treatment is available. But if they occur at home you should report them to your doctor at once.

Under no circumstances should an abortion be carried out by someone who is not medically qualified to carry out the operation. If the abortion has taken the form of scraping out the fetus, you should go home to bed, take things very easy for a couple of days, and abstain from intercourse while you are bleeding—which usually lasts five to ten days. If you suddenly get pains in the abdomen, a temperature, or much heavier bleeding, you should call a doctor right away and tell him what has happened.

If the abortion has been carried out by syringing the womb, you will usually, but not always, abort after twenty-four hours or so, and then not entirely painlessly.

Many women are shocked when they see how big the fetus is and how developed. By the end of the third month the fetus is about three inches long and already has head, body, arms, legs, fingers, and toes.

Together with the placenta it is about the size of an orange. This is something you obviously ought to know before you decide on an abortion.

When you have aborted it is sensible to ring the doctor, who will in most cases put you into the hospital. You should not refuse, since in a hospital you are under constant supervision and any complications can be treated immediately. Before you are discharged the hospital doctor will have verified whether it is necessary to scrape the womb (which it almost always is).

Superstitions

Many young women are seized with panic when they realize they are pregnant. And they may have good reason. They clutch at all kinds of "household remedies" or advice from friends in an attempt to provoke abortion. They leap about, go for motorcycle rides over ploughed fields, or try taking different medicines that are supposed to help.

But you should *not* believe any of these stories. Obviously some of the women who abort spontaneously have done something or other to provoke the abortion beforehand and when it happens they believe that it is because of what they have done, not knowing that they would have aborted anyway. In this way rumors are continually spread about some new wonder method, though none of them have any truth—not even the latest suggestion of taking fifty contraceptive pills at a time. Once the pregnancy has been confirmed, there is no substance, taken either orally or by injection, that will safely provoke an abortion without at the same time endangering the life of the woman who takes it.

If you take some kind of drug with the sole intention of causing an abortion and fail, you should consult your doctor before the ninth week of pregnancy. The drug may have harmed the fetus and it would be terrible to be responsible for handicaps in your child.

When a doctor induces an abortion, he syringes a solution of salt or sugar into the womb. But you must *never* try performing this operation on yourself, as it is very dangerous indeed. Since the solution must reach right inside the womb in order to be effective, it goes without saying that it is quite useless to try rinsing the vagina with it.

Before Birth

There are a number of situations in which a woman may bear a child but nevertheless be unwilling or unable to raise one. She may have a religious or moral objection to abortion, or she may have wanted a baby and changed her mind for some reason. If you feel you want to have your baby adopted there are a number of agencies that will help you. Planned Parenthood can provide prenatal care and/or adoption information. A Birthright or Lifeline office may offer counselling, referral, and perhaps financial aid, as will your local Catholic Charities office or Jewish Community Service office. (All of the above serve women of any faith.) You can also get in touch with a provate adoption agency. They will provide counselling, prenatal care, and financial aid, but you will not have to commit yourself until after the baby is born and the social worker assigned to you feels quite sure that *you* are sure about giving up your baby.

If you find you need total financial support, or if you decide to go to a home for unwed mothers after your pregnancy begins to show, you can get help from the state or local Department of Social Services, Public Assistance or Welfare.

There are many couples who are unable to have children of their own and are longing to bring up a baby. There is nothing disgraceful about having your child adopted. Nor need you worry that the baby will miss maternal feelings, since these will blossom in the adoptive mother.

It is important to think that these things through well before the baby is due, since arrangements have to be made for the care of the baby as soon as it is born. Even if you have agreed to have your baby adopted, you will be given time after the birth to make up your mind, so you need not worry that the baby will be taken away from you if you change your mind.

But for the child's sake it is essential to consider very carefully whether you are in a position to live up to the daily emotional demands imposed by a child. These needs are going to influence your way of life for a long time. Research has shown that a stable, emotional relationship is vital for the development of the child. Moreover, psychologists agree that the child should be adopted as early as possible, before it is six months old, since it has been observed that many children are psychologically damaged by changing their mother (or father) after this age.

So, if you are not sure that you can fill the constant demands of a child, if you feel that the child is an unwanted burden, it is best for you, but to an even greater extent for the child, to have it adopted.

13. Sexual Minority Groups

Certain forms of sexual display occur more frequently than others and are therefore called normal. But there is no scientific basis for drawing an exact dividing line between the normal and the abnormal and any attempt to do so is purely artificial and incidental. In fact it is purely a question of sliding over the boundaries between the usual, the less usual, and the highly unusual. Opinion varies as to whether the more unusual and exceptional forms of sexual behavior should be called abnormal or unhealthy. In any case the attitude that assumes that the "sexually normal" is also morally right, while the "sexually abnormal" is loathsome or morally reprehensible, seems very irrational.

In America, most people have been able to accept the fact that the sexual instinct is an elementary human instinct that needs satisfaction like any other. Even so, we try, both as individuals and as a society, to put obstacles in the way of sexual display among minority groups. We condemn them, repudiate them, and prosecute them with a totally unwarranted discrimination in the courts.

It may be useful to point out how hunger, another instinct, is satisfied in different ways around the world.

In China it is comman to eat dogs, while we would think our neighbor a "food pervert" if we saw him breeding dogs for this purpose. On the other hand, the Chinese do not eat dairy products, while we regard them as extremely healthy. Moreover, in England we eat a great deal of pork, whereas the Islamic religion forbids the consumption of pork.

For us eating people is one of the most disgusting and ghastly things imaginable, but many cannibalistic tribes see it as a beautiful and natural act. They believe that by eating particular parts of their fallen enemies or dead parents they assume the physical or spiritual strength of the dead person.

Altogether, there is hardly any form of good that is not considered agreeable somewhere in the world at the same time as being thought disgusting and nauseating elsewhere.

In the same way attitudes toward sexual behavior vary widely from society to society. What may be regarded as normal in one place is placed under strong taboos elsewhere. The difference is even more glaring when we go back in time. There have been societies in which what we call "abnormal" sexual display has been common practice in religious ceremonies: for example, incest, exposing the sex organs, homosexuality, sexual intercourse with animals, and coitus in public.

These things should show that our beliefs about what is sexually proper, just like our beliefs about what is proper food, are based first and foremost on culturally conditioned attitudes and on prejudices.

Just as we feel in our society that we have the right to satisfy our hunger, so too there should be a human right to have one's sexual impulses satisfied. Even if this satisfaction takes a form that we, either emotionally or rationally, take exception to. The only reasonable and necessary limit to impose on sexual behavior is that nobody be allowed to impose on another's mental or physical liberty.

Homosexuality

Homosexuality means that the sexual instinct is directed toward a person of the same sex. Both men and women can be homosexual, though when referring to homosexuality in women the expression *lesbian* love is often used.

A small percentage of adults are completely homosexual or lesbian, feeling sexually attracted only to members of their own sex and disgusted, to a greater or lesser degree, by the sex organs of the opposite sex. For them sexual attraction between people of different sexes is as emotionally incomprehensible as homosexuality can be for the nonhomosexual.

But the dividing lines are also flexible in this respect. Most of us are, in fact, more or less *bisexual;* that is, we can be attracted to either sex, often without thinking that there is anything sexual in it when we are attracted to members of our own sex. In the chapter on Masturbation we have talked of young men taking part in communal masturbation. So, at times, when it is impossible to achieve release from sexual urges toward the opposite sex, it is not unusual for homosexual methods to be used. This can happen at boarding schools, for example, in prisons, among soldiers, and so on.

In some cultures bisexuality has been not merely common, but also regarded as a beautiful form of expression. In ancient Greece, for example, men who had wives at home would have an affair with a young man during their leisure hours and also act as a kind of spiritual guardian to him. Among other people boys have had to undergo homosexual rituals with the men of the tribe as part of puberty ceremonies, in order to be accepted as adults.

In England homosexual relationships are illegal unless they take place between two adults over the age of twenty-one, no matter how keen the young man may have been to form the relationship in the first place. In comparison, it is possible for a man to have an affair with a girl over the age of sixteen, provided she has entered the relationship of her own free will.

This discrepancy is maintained on the ground that a man may be seduced into a lifetime of homosexuality if seduction takes place at such an early age that he had not yet had an affair with a member of the opposite sex. But these grounds have long since been rejected as false by various leading psychiatrists, so it is hard to see why they should influence the laws. For they lead to inhumanitarian treatment of homosexual men, since they then become easy prey for "male prostitutes," that is, young men who offer themselves to homosexuals for money. In most cases they are not completely homosexual themselves but are only doing it for the cash. A male prostitute can make serious trouble for a homosexual partner by leading him to believe that he is over the age of consent. The situation may be exploited by the prostitute who is tempted to blackmail and sometimes even to commit physical violence and theft against the homosexual, who dares not go to the police.

In the United States, almost all states maintain laws against sodomy; these forbid any kind of sexual intercourse other than genital-to-genital. Although sodomy laws and laws against sex in public places frequently apply to certain heterosexual practices as well as to homosexual acts, they are nearly always used against homosexuals. Homosexuals are also discriminated against in housing, employment, and in the armed services. For more information about local laws affecting homosexuals and/or social services for homosexuals, contact the Mattachine Society (see page 142).

In many cases ordinary young people are disparaging about homosexuals. And sometimes young men react with irrational brutality when they are exposed to homosexual advances.

There is no denying that many homosexuals are unhappy about their sexual characteristics and that young people who have experienced their first sexual climax in this way may be worried about becoming homosexual, that is, living the life of a homosexual with persecution and intolerance from the people around him. But luckily there are many homosexuals who succeed in finding partners of a similar disposition with whom they can live a secure and satisfactory life. However, it is extremely rare that a complete homosexual has any interest at all in becoming heterosexual, even should the possibility exist. Homosexuals are content with their sexual characteristics and wish only for more understanding and equality of rights in the eyes of society, so that they can live in the way they find most satisfying without fear.

There is no known medical remedy that can change homosexuality to heterosexuality (sexual relations between opposite sexes), but some homosexuals have so much of the bisexual in them that a psychiatrist or psychoanalyst can change the direction of their sexual impulses through prolonged psychoanalytic treatment.

Exhibitionists

An exhibitionist is a person who feels a desire to expose his sexual organs to total strangers in public places.

122

In most cases he will be a man who hides behind a tree or a gateway and then steps out with his trousers unbuttoned and exhibits his penis when some unsuspecting woman appears. The fright he provokes in the woman is sometimes an essential sexual stimulus that can cause him to have an erection, if he hasn't already got one. Ejaculation usually follows soon after, quite often without his even needing to masturbate. He is continually afraid of being arrested and has usually planned his escape route carefully, but while his body is sexually excited his desire to run away will be kept in check. Usually, as soon as he has finished his orgasm he will be seized with fear and rush off.

Of course it can be unpleasant for a young girl to encounter an exhibitionist—after all it is always unpleasant to be given a shock—but there is absolutely no reason to panic. An exhibitionist does *only* what we have described. He is not interested in intercourse, as a rule he is impotent in situations where intercourse might be expected, and he is so apprehensive and so ready to run away himself that he won't even dare try to get close to the woman. If a woman encourages him instead of being frightened, he will run away.

Peeping Toms (Voyeurs)

Almost all men are Peeping Toms in the sense that they enjoy watching a woman undressing—hence the success of striptease dancers. It is not until the desire to do this determines the way in which an individual person satisfies his sexual urges that one can start talking about it as a sexual characteristic. Usually voyeurs are men who try to watch other people undressing or making love through cracks and windows. Sometimes they masturbate as they watch.

Some people may find it embarrassing and disagreeable to know that they are being watched. Other people with more exhibitionistic tendencies may feel, on the contrary, sexually stimulated by such knowledge. Usually, however, the watched are not aware of the watcher—and what you don't know you can't worry about.

The law is unreasonably hard on both exhibitionists and voyeurs, who can be given prison sentences for their possibily embarrassing but harmless and humble pleasures. So you ought to think twice before involving the police. If you don't like seeing a man exposing his sex organs you can turn your head the other way and walk past—he won't do anything else. And if you don't care for the idea of being watched, then try not to tempt the voyeur unnecessarily by not drawing your curtains properly and so on. If you are unlucky enough to come up behind an exhibitionist or a voyeur and surprise him in the act, then surely it is most humanitarian to withdraw discreetly. After all, you would hate the idea of being disturbed in a sexual situation yourself and you do not risk being prosecuted.

Sexual Intercourse with Animals (Bestiality, Zoophilia)

By this we understand that men and women satisfy their sexual impulses with the help of animals, most often in intercourse.

Zoophilia is considerably more widespread than one usually imagines. Kinsey found an average of 8 percent of men and 4 percent of women who had had sexual experiences of this kind, and in country districts 17 percent of the male population had experienced orgasm with an animal.

In this country it is *illegal* to satisfy your sexual urges in this way.

Such contact between animals and humans cannot —as was once believed—result in conception.

Incest

By this we mean sexual relations between adults and their children or grandchildren and between brothers and sisters. Sexual intercourse between such close relatives is illegal in this country.

The taboo against this form of sexual activity used to be waived during certain religious ceremonies in several cultures, and in some species of animals, incest is a normal phenomenon. In pedigree breeding it is a common method of keeping the strain as pure as possible. On the other hand, inbreeding can result in increased chances of bad hereditary characteristics being passed to the next generation. It is probably an awareness of this that is behind the taboo on incest in human beings.

Sadism—Masochism

A sadist is a person who can be sexually stimulated only by hurting (whipping, for example) another person and a masochist is a person who has to be hurt to achieve the same result.

Sadists and masochists are to be found equally among homosexuals and heterosexuals. Quite often a person can be a sadist and a masochist at the same time.

Many people show streaks of sadism or masochism in their loveplay, but there is no question of demonstrating an actual sexual characteristic unless these streaks have become a necessary condition of sexual stimulation or satisfaction and are taken to excess.

Pedophiles (Child Molesters)

Pedophiles are people who need to caress the sex organs of a child and who often also wish the child to touch theirs. Such a method of achieving sexual satisfaction is considered "indecent" and is punishable by prison sentences.

As a rule, however, "enticers" are kindly people who treat the children tenderly and affectionately and the child's natural sexual curiosity may find an outlet in the company of the pedophile. If the child lacks warmth and love in his or her own home, the recognition of such feelings in the "enticer" will make him or her feel secure and comfortable in his company.

Only rarely will a pedophile be intent on performing intercourse with a little girl. Apart from such cases he is as harmless as those female pedophiles about whom one hears little because their activities are considered harmless by society.

Obviously children must be protected against violent assault. But this should not be done by scaring them out of their wits with nasty stories about "bad men," since they are bound to react with anxious screams if they are enticed to some out-of-the-way place, thus frightening the man, who had no desire to have intercourse with them, into taking some drastic action to prevent discovery.

Instead children should be taught not to go with strangers, even if these people offer them sweets or toys. This is not because the men wish them any harm, but because they want to do something grown-up with them, which they, the children, are still too little for. Of course it is even better to tell the children what it is all about in a relaxed way, but this presupposes that they are already well informed about sexual matters.

Rape

Rape is an act of "unlawful, forcible sexual intercourse." A man rapes a girl or woman by forcing his penis into her vagina, her mouth, or her anus. A man rapes a boy or man by forcing his penis into the other's mouth or anus. He may use actual force or violence, or he may threaten to; either way, it is still rape. After a rape, the victim should call the police immediately, and not wash or bathe or attempt to clean up until after being examined by a doctor. Cuts and bruises, torn flesh or clothing, and the presence of semen in the vagina or anus will be the victim's only proof that rape has occurred, and unfortunately the vast majority of rapists go unpunished because the crime is not reported correctly or not reported at all.

14. Diseases and Other Problems

VENEREAL DISEASES

These are contagious diseases that are spread almost exclusively through sexual contact.

The main venereal diseases are gonorrhea (pronounced gonoreea), nonspecific urethritis, and syphilis, and these, if not treated, can lead to disablement later on. During the last ten years there has been a gradual increase in the number of cases of venereal disease, especially of gonorrhea, and it is thought that this increase is chiefly due to more liberal sexual attitudes among young people.

Sooner or later some of you will enter into sexual relations with loose-living people. Then it is wise to watch out for the symptoms of venereal disease, as described below, and if you have the least suspicion that you have contracted anything, go to the doctor at once. That way you will avoid the disease establishing itself and infecting other people.

The doctor will either treat you himself or send you to a treatment center. If you prefer not to consult your doctor you can go to a special clinic. Most general hospitals have such clinics. You will be treated with complete anonymity and given a number instead of being referred to by your name. Although you are not obliged to name the person from whom you have caught the disease, it is obviously wise, if you know them, to make sure that they know they are infected so that they have treatment too.

Gonorrhea (Clap)

Gonorrhea is the most common form of venereal disease. The first symptoms in both men and women are noticeable two to eight days after infection and take the form of an itching or smarting sensation in the urethra that becomes worse when you pass water. After the first few days a mucous secretion appears from the opening to the urethra. This discharge becomes stronger and more yellowish in color over the following days and is a sign that the infection has spread further up into the urethra.

Even if you do not ask for treatment the symptoms may disappear of their own accord. Indeed some people have no outward symptoms at all. But this does not mean that you are cured; the disease will just spread up into the sex organs unnoticed. Then, after a while, it breaks out again in the form of a malignant infection of the prostate gland or the balls in men and an infection of the abdomen in women. This can result in sterility, or an inability to have children, in both sexes. If you still don't get any treatment the disease may spread to the main joints (very often the knee joints) and eventually to the heart and other vital organs.

Usually gonorrhea is contracted *only* through sexual contact, though anyone who has the disease must exercise great cleanliness and remember in particular to wash their hands after touching their sex organs, since the infection can be passed from the hands to another person's genitals. In this respect there are several recorded cases of mothers and nurses who have transmitted the disease to children while dressing or washing them.

Nonspecific Urethritis (N.S.U.)

Almost as common as gonorrhea is nonspecific urethritis (given this name because doctors are not agreed on what causes it). In clinical appearance N.S.U. in men is rather like gonorrhea and the treatment is similar. There are no obvious symptoms in women, but anyone who has had sexual contact with a man affected by N.S.U. should go to a V.D. clinic for examination and advice.

Syphilis (Pox)

Syphilis is the most serious form of venereal disease, and if it isn't treated can develop into one of the most terrible diseases in existence, though with the progress of medical science advanced syphilis is gradually becoming rarer. Unlike gonorrhea, syphilis can also be contracted by kissing and the disease can even be transmitted from inanimate objects such as infected lavatory seats, but this is very rare.

Two to six weeks (usually three weeks) after infection, the first stage of the disease sets in with a little sore (hard chancre) on the place where the infection was transmitted—most frequently on the genitals, but fairly often on the lips, in the mouth, on the fingers, or in other areas that have been in contact with the infection. This sore is hard, firm, and *almost completely insensitive*, which is why one may be inclined not to take it seriously. Even if the disease is not treated, the sore will disappear over a couple of weeks, but this does *not* mean that you are cured. This disease then spreads steadily but unnoticed over the body. After some months it breaks out again in what is known as the second stage. This usually takes the form of a rash of red spots over the whole body and swelling in all the glands, though this swelling is most noticeable in the armpits, the groin, and on the sides of the neck. At this stage some people get blisters in their mouth and a few begin to lose their hair. Even these symptoms need not seem unduly serious to the person who has the disease, though they will certainly worry, and again they will disappear without any kind of treatment. For the next ten to twenty years the sufferer may feel quite healthy but eventually the disease breaks out again. This third stage is extremely serious and potentially fatal, since it can affect the heart, the nervous system, and the brain (leading to insanity).

Other Forms of Venereal Disease

It is possible to contract through intercourse a virus infection that manifests itself in the form of soft, whitish, wartlike spots. These may not appear until two or three months after infection. It is important to have them removed while they are small, since they can grow and become persistent.

Venereal ulcers are sores on the genitals that may be accompanied by swelling in the groin. This disease is so rare in our part of the world that a more detailed account of it seems superfluous.

Protection against Venereal Disease

If you use a condom throughout intercourse you are protected against gonorrhea and to a certain extent against syphilis—a fact which many prostitutes discovered some time ago, which is why they will quite often demand that their "clients" use a condom during intercourse.

It is common practice, particularly among sailors, to rub calomel ointment on the skin on and around their sex organs immediately after intercourse in situations where there is a certain risk of catching syphilis. But, though this method is better than nothing, it does not give complete safety.

OTHER DISEASES AND AFFLICTIONS

Bad Breath

By this we mean that one's exhalations have an unpleasant smell. If bad breath persists without getting any better even though you brush your teeth rigorously every morning and evening, it usually means, in young people, that they have cavities in their teeth, something wrong with their tonsils, or incrustation of the nostrils. So the only thing to do is first to go to the dentist and, if that doesn't help, to an ear, nose, and throat specialist (on the recommendation of your doctor).

Growth in the Balls

If one of your balls suddenly begins to grow, you must go and see your doctor, even if they do not feel tender or painful. It might be due to a rupture or cyst in the scrotum (in which case it isn't actually the testicle that is growing, though it feels like it), but it might also be due to a malignant tumor in the testicle that must be removed by an operation as soon as possible.

Missing Balls

In small boys it is fairly common to find that one or both of the balls have not descended into the scrotum. This means that the ball will not function properly and a doctor should be consulted right away, since it has proved necessary to operate before the child is five years old, otherwise the growth and development of the undescended testicle may be impaired. It is also possible for one of the balls to slip up into the groin, especially if the scrotum is under pressure. In such cases you should also see a doctor, who will be able to press it gently down again.

Pain in the Balls

The balls are often very sensitive. You may even faint from the pain of a strong kick or blow directed at them.

Any disease that makes the balls swell, like gonorrhea or mumps, will usually cause pain (though see also under Growth in the Balls).

Varicose veins in the small blood vessels around the spermatic cord may result in pain while you are running or engaged in vigorous exercise. The pains will then disappear when you are sitting still. You may find that it helps to lift up the scrotum in tight-fitting underpants or to strap it in a suspensory bandage especially made for this purpose. If this doesn't relieve the pain sufficiently then you can have a small operation to remove the varicose vein.

Some people may get pains in the balls if they are sexually excited for a long period of time without reaching a climax. An ejaculation, by whatever means it is achieved, will ease the condition.

Blood in the Semen

Very rarely you may find streaks of blood in the semen—after masturbation, for example. This is usually an indication that some small blood vessel has

133

burst, which need not worry you. But it may be due to some much more serious disease. So you should let the doctor examine you to make sure all is well.

Crab Lice

Crab lice live in the hair around the genitals and are therefore generally transmitted by intercourse. A crab louse can become dislodged, however, and fall onto an infected lavatory seat, for example, to take up residence in the next person who uses the lavatory. The lice suck blood and produce small blue marks and itching.

Crab lice will not go away no matter how thoroughly you wash and bathe. You will have to get a special solution sold by the druggist. You should wet the hair round the sex organs and under the arms thoroughly with the liquid, stop washing these parts for the next five days, and the cure will take effect.

Foreskin Infections

So much smegma and urine can collect under the foreskin, particularly among men who suffer from tightness of the foreskin, that it becomes infected. The foreskin grows red and swollen, it supurates, tickles, and smarts. If you keep yourself clean under the foreskin you can avoid irritations of this kind, but obviously if the foreskin is tight it may be impossible to wash yourself properly.

Infection in the foreskin usually needs treatment from a doctor.

Tightness of the Foreskin

If the foreskin fits so closely that it cannot easily be drawn back over the head of the penis, you are suffering from phimosis, or tightness of the foreskin. Almost all little boys have phimosis without there being anything abnormal about it—by far the majority of them grow out of it. If you are well into puberty and the foreskin still isn't any looser you should go to the doctor—you must *not* try to force it back yourself. All that is needed is a small operation known as circumcision, which is performed on many small boys in certain societies, is very common in America, and is a religious practice among Jews, for example.

Hair Growth

Some girls are bothered by a vigorous growth of hair on the arms, legs, and face. If the hair grows slowly and gradually, it is a hereditary characteristic and you can remove it as described on page 5. If the hair grows very thickly, or appears suddenly—possibly in conjunction with other irregularities—it may be because you are suffering from some hormonal disorder, in which case it is advisable to consult a doctor.

Impurities of the Skin

You may be plagued by spots and pimples for several years. It is hardly any consolation to be told that they will disappear of their own accord as time goes by because while you have them you may be feeling so unattractive and repulsive that it's enough to give you a "complex."

There are different ways of tackling the problem, but a combination of all the remedies usually gives the best results.

Your *diet* is important: fruit, vegetables, lean meat, fish, skimmed or butter milk, and low-fat cheeses will all help to clear the skin. Dairy-fat products—like butter, milk, cream, chocolate and ice cream—eggs, and fatty meat are all spot-makers. So it is better to fry food in oil or vegetable margarine than in butter, since vegetable products, with a few exceptions such as nuts, have fewer repercussions in this respect.

Fresh air, sunshine, and salt water dry out spots and greasy skin. In winter a sun-ray lamp may prove a good substitute for these.

Daily attention to the skin may also be necessary. Do try to avoid picking at your spots even though you're itching to. Then, when the pimple is large and yellow you can carefully squeeze it out in a wad of cotton wool. Wash your skin with some kind of medicated soap (the bacteria killer hexachlorophene can be prescribed for this) by massaging the soap carefully into the skin and leaving it a minute before rinsing. This should be done daily or it won't help at all. Never use propyl alcohol, ether, and things like that to cleanse the skin, as these substances just remove the protective layer of fat on the skin and may even cause the spots to spread.

Blackheads are produced by the waxy wastage of the sebaceous glands. If they are allowed to remain on the skin too long they become large and dark. Before you attempt to remove the blackheads with your fingers you should wash both them and your skin with medicated soap for at least a minute, otherwise there is a danger of a spot forming in the hole left when the blackhead is removed.

Inverted Nipples

Some women have inverted nipples. In most cases this will make breast-feeding very difficult when you have a baby, and you may also find inverted nipples unattractive to look at. The problem can be helped by massage—you should ask your doctor how to do this. Otherwise it may be necessary to perform a small plastic surgery operation.

Menstrual Difficulties and Pains

A certain number of girls have a fair amount of trouble with their periods during the days before they are due or when they start. This may consist of puffiness in the face, a feeling of tightness in the breasts, pains in the abdomen, and aching joints.

And you may be affected mentally, suffering from restlessness, lack of tolerance, and exaggerated irritation over trivia.

Usually this disappears in the course of a few years, though this is small comfort to those who suffer from such troubles.

Some form of hormone treatment, for example, the Pill (see page 106) often alleviates the symptoms or gets rid of them altogether, so talk to your doctor about it.

Menstrual Irregularities

The first year a girl has her period they may be very irregular without there being anything abnormal. Emotional upsets, travelling, and pregnancy fears can make you miss your period several times. If it hasn't sorted itself out by the time you are eighteen you should consult your doctor.

Scabies

Scabies is caused by a tiny, almost invisible mite that lives in small burrows under the skin, particularly between the fingers, around the waist, and in the armpits. The symptom of scabies is a powerful itch.

Scabies is often transmitted by sexual relations,

when the bodies of two people are lying close to one another, but you can also catch it by holding hands or using other people's clothes or bed.

Scabies can be cured by applying a special solution that you can buy at a drugstore. After your bath, spread the stuff all over the body (except on the head) thoroughly. You should not wash until twenty-four hours later. You must also change your sheets and underclothes. It is wise to repeat this cure four to five days later.

Smarting Pains when Urinating

Mention has already been made of the fact that one of the first symptoms of gonorrhea is smarting when passing water.

These stinging pains, together with a frequent need to urinate, can also be a sign of an infection of the bladder. Both these conditions require medical help.

However, young women may also need to urinate more often, and have stinging pains when they do, after they first have intercourse, without there being any question of disease. It is due to irritation of the urethra after unaccustomed pressure. It will disappear after a few days without any treatment. It used to be called "honeymoon cystitis," with humorous overtones.

Soreness in the Womb

Some women may have pains in the lower abdomen if the penis reaches deep inside them during intercourse. The womb can be tender during the days before a period. Usually it doesn't mean anything at all, but if you always feel pain in the womb during intercourse the trouble may be more serious. You may have a sore on the cervix, your womb may be tilted backward, or—especially if you also have some discharge—it may be due to some kind of infection. Then you should definitely seek medical advice.

Pains during intercourse may also be due to psychological difficulties for which psychological or psychiatric help should be sought.

Sweating Tendencies

During puberty many young people are bothered by heavy sweating. Clean sweat does not smell nasty, but there are bacteria on the skin that can reduce sweat to an evil-smelling component very quickly.

If you wash the parts that sweat most for at least a minute every day with a soap containing the bacteria-killing substance hexachlorophene (most medicated soaps contain this ingredient) you can prevent the sweaty smell, because the soap leaves a layer of bacteria killer on the skin.

Vaginal Discharge

During the first years of puberty it is quite common for girls to have a small amount of thin, whitish, nonsmelling discharge from the vagina. It can be a nuisance, but as a rule there is nothing to be done. It is certainly not due to any disease. The worst thing you can do is rinse the vagina with a douche. This will just increase the discharge. You should also stop using tampons during your periods, as these can irritate the membrane and make the situation worse.

If the discharge becomes more creamy and yellowish and there is more of it, then it may be a sign of some kind of fungus, or a bacterial or parasitic growth in the vagina. Your doctor will be able to prescribe suppositories to cure such a condition.

These suppositories are inserted into the vagina for about twelve nights running.

A strong, evil-smelling, greenish-yellowish-brownish discharge can be a sign of a much more serious infection, especially if such a discharge is accompanied by pains and a temperature. In this case you should consult your doctor immediately.

Information on Services

For All Services

If you need a specific medical service (or think you might), or advice about finding a doctor in your area who will treat you confidentially, or if you want to locate a counsellor or a rap group to talk about things that trouble you, contact your nearest Planned Parenthood office. If you don't find one listed in the telephone book, call Information in the larger cities near you. Even if they are too far away for you to get to, they may be able to direct you to a community sex education service or family planning clinic. If you can't locate a Planned Parenthood office nearby, call the national headquarters in New York City and they will direct you. The number is (212) 541-7800.

For Unplanned Pregnancy

If you have decided that you want an abortion, or if you want counselling to help you with your decision, or if you want specific information about getting an abortion in your area, you can check the phone book and/or Information for the Clergy Consultation Service. If you can't locate an office nearby, the national headquarters will direct you; call (212) 477-0034.

Sex Information

If you have a question about anything to do with sex, the following organizations maintain hot lines to try to answer them:

IN NEW YORK CITY:

The Community Sex Information Service
P. O. Box 2858, Grand Central Station
New York, N.Y. 10017
(212) 586-6666

You can also write them, but they advise that they can understand and answer your questions better if they talk to you. Call from 7 to 9 P.M., Monday through Thursday.

IN BOSTON:
The Community Sex Information Service
(617) 232-2335

IN SAN FRANCISCO:
The San Francisco Sex Information Service
(415) 665-7300

Unfortunately none of the numbers above is toll-free, nor can the organizations afford to accept collect calls. But your health and peace of mind are worth the investment. And don't be shy—there's nothing you can ask them that they haven't heard before, and if they were going to be judgmental, they wouldn't have gone into the counselling business.

Venereal Disease

If you need information, or want to know where to get V.D. tests or treatment in your area, you can call Operation Venus in Philadelphia toll-free from 9 A.M. to 9 P.M. The number is (800) 523-1885.

Sexual Minority Groups

The Mattachine Society functions as a national clearinghouse for helping homosexuals help and protect each other. They will provide information on local laws affecting homosexuals and the names and addresses of local homosexual activist groups. The address is

Mattachine Society
59 Christopher Street
New York, New York 10014

Index

Page numbers in boldface indicate subject headings. Italics indicate illustrations.

future kinds of, 107–108
Pimples, 6, **135**
Planned Parenthood, 100, 110, 116, 141
Pornography, ix, 36
Pox. *See* Syphilis
Pregnancy, 7, 24, 53, 60, 115
  and abortion, 110–116
  first signs of, **109**
  test for, 109–110
Prostrate gland, 5, *28*
Puberty, xiii, **3**, 40
Pubic bone, *22*, *28*, 67, 77, *98*
Pubic hair. *See* Hair, growth of

Rape, **127**
Rectum, *22*, *28*
Responsibility, 40
Retroverted womb, 89

Sadism, **125**
Sanitary napkins, 26
Scabies, **137**
Scrotum, 5, **27**, 69, 132
Self, 10
Self-abuse, 31
Self-gratification, 31–32
Semen, 7, 24, **28**, 34, 57, 58, 70–71, 80, 88, 94, 107
Seminal ducts, 26, 27
Seminal fluid, 27
Seminal vesicles, 5, 27, *28*
Services, information on, **141**
Sex organs, 5
  female, **19**, *20*, *22*
  male, **26**, *28*
Sexual Behavior in the Human Female, x
Sexual Behavior in the Human Male, x
Sexual Behaviour of Young People, The, ix
Sexual dreams. *See* Dreams, erotic
Sexual fantasies, **35**, 68
Sexual maturity, 3, **7**, 15–17, 88
Smegma, 27, **134**
Sodomy, laws against, 121
Sperm, 24, 91
Sperm cells, 27, 29, 89, 94, 107

Spermatic cord, 5
Spermatic duct, 26, *28*, 107
Spermicidal creams, **91**, 99
Spermicidal jelly, 74
Spermicidal suppositories, **91**, 96
Spermicidal sprays, 91–92, 96
Spots. *See* Pimples
Sprays, 91, 96
Sterility, 114
Stimulants, erotic, 47–51
Suckling, 5
Syphilis, **130**

Tampons, 19, 26
Technical virgins, 60
Testicles (balls), 5, 26, **27**, *28*, 69
  missing, **132**
  pain in, 41, **133**
Twins, **24**

Urethra, 19, *20*, *22*, *28*, 69, 70, 129
  smarting pain in, 138
Urethritis, nonspecific, **130**
Urine test, 109
Uterus. *See* Womb

Vagina, 6, 19, *20*, 21, *22*, 24–26, 30, 49, 55, 57, 58, 62, 65, 73–74, 78, 83, *98*
Vaginal cramps, 74
Vaginal discharge, **139**
Vaginism, 74
Varicose veins, 60, 133
Vas deferens, 26
Vaseline, 60, 94
V.D. *See* Venereal diseases
Venereal diseases, 92, 97, **128**
Venereal ulcers, 131
Virgin. *See* Technical virgin
Virginity, 53, 58, 60
Voice, breaking of, 4
Voyeur. *See* Peeping Toms

Wet dreams, 7
Womb, 6, 21–25, *22*, 66
  soreness in, 74, **138**

Zoophilia, **124**

145

About the Authors

BENT H. CLAËSSON. Born 1935. Doctor since 1963. On staff of various hospitals and institutions, including psychiatic departments. Has given sex education classes to the young and in spring 1968 took part in the radio series, "Love as a School Subject," and has since appeared on many radio and television programs on sex education.

GREGERS NIELSEN. Born 1931. 1948 junior on local paper in Fyen. Free-lance work at home and abroad. 1964 started Delta Photos with Jesper Hom. Has done photography for several books and short films and exhibited in Denmark and elsewhere.